CATALYST

How Accountants Can Be the Agents of Change in the Net Zero Transition

James Lizars FCCA

Copyright Page

First published in Great Britain in 2025

by JEL Impact Media Ltd

CONTENTS

DEDICATION

For Josh and Genevieve,

because your future depends on the choices we make now.

Ours may be the last generation with the chance to change the story,

but also the one with the greatest hope and opportunity to do so.

May you inherit a world still brimming with possibility.

xxx

FOREWORD

By Helen Brand OBE

Chief executive, ACCA (Association of Chartered Certified Accountants)

Imagine your country has reached the final of the football World Cup.

The coach gathers the players in the dressing room just before they go out to play Brazil and announces that only the goalkeeper, the left-back, the right winger, and the centre-forward will start the game. The manager says they can win the match with only half the side, and everyone else can stay in the changing room.

That's pretty much where we are with climate change and the Green Transition in business right now.

It's by far the biggest challenge facing us – yet most of business remains on the sidelines of the action needed to turn the tide on global warming and reshape our economies along sustainable lines.

That's because the focus of Governments and standards setters is on the actions of the biggest businesses. It flies in the face of the facts that Small and Medium Sized Enterprises (SMEs) account for 90% of the world's firms, 50% of the global workforce and 50% of business greenhouse gas emissions.

I know that SMEs are ready, eager and able to play their full part in finding solutions to the greatest problems facing our world and unlock fresh opportunities in this fast-expanding sector.

I also know that the accountants who work with these businesses are anxious and willing to help their clients make their best contribution.

And that is where the true, exceptional value of James' book lies – in preparing accountants to serve as faithful and diligent advisers on every aspect of the Green Transition that is becoming a bigger part of business life.

Of course, it's a commercial question as much as it is a moral and an ethical question.

It's a question of risk, and accountants can mitigate risk by bringing the skills and knowledge to guide SME clients through an often tangled and confused maze of reporting requirements. It's a growing necessity and the price of staying in business for SMEs, as regulation extends from big businesses down through their supply chains.

Increasingly, SMEs need to provide assurance that their operations comply with their corporate customers' reporting needs. Smaller concerns don't always have the resources to hire that level of specialism in-house. They need expert guidance from their professional accountant to navigate choppy waters.

James also explains how the sustainability agenda brings new opportunities for accountants to carry out new work in new fields and win new business from SME clients who are increasingly interested and involved in the arena of the Green Transition.

These are all compelling reasons why James's book is such a welcome and timely contribution to a critical issue, and I am delighted to say that accountants couldn't have a better guide.

I know James from his service on ACCA's governing Council, and his concerns about the burning need for a sharper focus on sustainability in business were always ahead of their time. I am so pleased that the global agenda has now caught up with the necessary urgency in this field.

Like all ACCA accountants, James is a deeply practical individual. He seeks solutions, not just fine-sounding words. In that sense, this book is a valuable, pragmatic and indispensable guide for any accountant who works in the SME sector.

It will play a major part in ensuring that as we face the toughest business challenge we have ever faced, we will enter the field with a full-strength team.

INTRODUCTION

Let me state from the outset that this is not a book about the climate crisis.

It's about net zero.

Now, I realise net zero isn't unrelated to the climate crisis. Still, my intention in the following chapters is to explain what net zero is and isolate it from the range of narratives that exist around climate change, especially the spectrum of opinion that is projected at us, often angrily. It's not such a strange ambition as it might first sound because net zero is a very particular concept enshrined in law in the UK and many other countries around the world.

So, while I am deeply concerned about the future as an individual and as a parent, I'm not a climate scientist. I'm not qualified to speak to the science other than to say that I accept what the United Nations Intergovernmental Panel on Climate Change (IPCC) and many others tell us. We have a profound and urgent need to decarbonise our lifestyles, businesses, and economies, and the core mechanism for doing so is net zero.

As a chartered certified accountant who works in practice advising Small and Medium-sized businesses (SMEs), and as a business owner myself, I look at the fact of net zero, of the enormous economic transition that sits behind it and wonder, *When do we ever get such foresight of a major shift in the business context?* We had no choice but to react to the COVID-19 pandemic, the Credit Crunch, the Dotcom Bubble and every other recession. We don't know the endpoint for the internet revolution, smartphones, globalisation, AI. However, with net zero, there is a shift that will provide context over the coming **decades,** with the aim to achieve net zero carbon emissions by 2050, including near-term targets along the way. And like any major economic shift, it can be disastrous for a business that fails to act, whereas early action can unlock opportunities.

Don't get me wrong. My natural instinct here isn't to rub my hands and highlight the ways in which net zero can be exploited to unlock riches beyond your wildest dreams. My aim is to show you the business case for profound and urgent action. To equip you to act upon that in your business and empower you to add net zero into your business advisory toolkit, should you wish to.

What is net zero?

A generally accepted definition would be that net zero means reducing greenhouse gas emissions as much as possible and balancing any remaining emissions by removing an equivalent amount from the atmosphere, ensuring no overall contribution to global warming.

When I first looked into the topic in 2019, as the owner of a small, digital-first, (virtually) paperless accounting business, my initial thought was that however much emissions reduction we achieved, our real-term impact would be so small as to be pointless.

However, I knew I needed to somehow do my bit on climate action, so I challenged myself on what that meant to me. What did it mean to 'do my bit'? I started with a tree planting and offsets subscription, notionally offsetting the impact of our team since that provided a near-instant outcome. It also felt good, perhaps similar to making a charitable donation.

But with emissions reductions, my first impression was that it sounded more like a set of difficult-to-achieve, do-good gestures that would have little impact on the real world. And much of the information I could find online sounded confusing and heavy on the jargon. I felt like I was just scratching the surface, but the more I went down the rabbit hole, it became apparent that beneath the noise, there was, in fact, a whole bank of knowledge I needed to get my head around if our business was to achieve net zero.

I soon discovered that net zero is an entire, dynamic world in its own right that's evolving in parallel to the more narrowly focused world I operated in. Constantly in flux with swathes of new regulations being drafted, it can be bewildering to a novice or the unprepared, particularly for SMEs, because so much thinking and legislation relates to big business.

On that basis, my challenge was to identify what this all meant for small businesses and whether any of the measures required to reduce greenhouse gases (GHG) differed from anything asked of me as a householder. Business owners and businesses are so interlinked at the smaller end of the spectrum. Our company was already paperless, except for the **endless** brown envelopes from HMRC, which we dutifully recycle.

What else?

What other personal sacrifices do they (whoever 'they' are) want me to make to help save the planet?

Except, of course, personal sacrifice or lifestyle change is the domestic side of the conversation. It's become politicised. It's a wedge issue. It's a source of division. And it has little or nothing to do with running a small business. It's simply more noise around the subject of net zero.

However, when net zero is framed in a business context, it soon becomes apparent that it surrounds a profoundly different set of issues. These issues will have a direct impact on business benefits, opportunities, and risks and could ultimately threaten a business's continuing existence.

In fact, it's beginning to look like a SWOT analysis. As an accountant, that's very familiar territory. If I could approach net zero utilising all my skills and expertise within that kind of framework, then perhaps it's not just noise; it's more a source of business insight.

That power of insight is the key driver behind writing this book for accountants and bookkeepers. We need to be increasingly aware of the measures and mitigations required to meet net zero so that we can all prepare our businesses and clients to be as sustainable as possible. The good news is we don't need to bury our heads in books and learn about the science because we already have a range of hidden superpowers to meet the challenge. Those superpowers are our skills, expertise, code of ethics and abilities to analyse data, identify opportunities and forecast potential outcomes. Nor is it just about sustainability; it's also about identifying unexpected areas of growth. Mapping out a net zero pathway sounds like a job for finance professionals to me.

I want you to feel as empowered about net zero as I do. My imagination was first caught in 2019 at a conference for members of B1G1, a micro-giving platform focused on achieving the UN Sustainable Development Goals (SDGs), where each of the 200 delegates shared the same passionate value – business as a force for good. One speaker stood out in particular; he shared that his speaker career involved dozens of international flights per annum. That got him thinking that he could offset the greenhouse gas (GHG) impact of those flights if he were to plant X trees. His challenge to us in the room was, given that this was a low-cost exercise, why didn't we all commit to offset the equivalent of the row in front and behind us whenever we took a flight? That would equate to a 10x offset per person of our own flights using trees. My reaction was instant and instinctive because it lacked direct equivalence. Trees take forever to grow! It seemed to me this was a fundamental misunderstanding of the nature of carbon offsets. *How was* this *room of progressive business leaders being given* this *pitch?*

This was the key trigger for me to start my net zero journey. Supporting wide-ranging B1G1 projects targeting various SDGs, I resolved to focus on Goal 13 - Climate Action. I was keen to know what net zero would look like for my business and how I could move the agenda along. It also led me eventually towards the Million Tree Pledge[1] and overplanting to continue drawing down CO_2 long past

[1] To learn more about how a group of individuals and businesses came together and committed to planting over 1 million trees each in response to the Climate Emergency visit https://www.milliontreepledge.org/

2050, and ultimately writing this book, which is the natural extension of my curiosity.

It's written specifically with the likes of you and me in mind - accountants and bookkeepers who work for or with SMEs. My mission is to cut through the noisy, crowded spaces that suffocate net zero as a subject matter.

The following chapters are a walkthrough of what net zero means (and doesn't mean) and the impact of regulations. The information I share will equip you with everything you need to know so that you can speak from a point of authority with your colleagues and clients to convince them that this is important for business. It's also a numbers game that you can perhaps monetise, and all that takes is having a basic understanding of what net zero really represents and then translating that into your pre-existing skill set and toolkit. And, once you're better equipped to explain the business case that identifies the risks of inaction, coupled with the opportunities for additional revenue streams and growth, that's perhaps all you'll need to help make that net zero journey a reality.

CHAPTER 1

NET ZERO MISCONCEPTIONS

What is Net zero? We've looked at a general definition, and it seems obvious, right?

Nope.

The reality is net zero's meaning is anything but obvious. Think about how a room of accountants might individually calculate the value of a business, and you get the idea of how nuanced it could be. So, whilst awareness is high, knowledge is low. Or at least lower than it ought to be, which includes SMEs, and that's fair enough. Life is tough running an SME business, and the priority list is seemingly endless as it is. Does this mean we have to do all of the normal stuff and learn to be green, too?

It can feel like a two-pronged assault. One from external voices imploring us to take action because of **all the bad stuff**. And increasingly from within our own value chains where larger corporate or public sector customers create a trickle-down impact on the supply chain as they pursue their own net zero commitments. In all probability, this impacts your business, if not immediately, then certainly at some point in the not-too-distant future.

Anything less than being prepared to meet this challenge head-on can spell economic disaster for SMEs that mistakenly believe they've either done enough or, more likely, are mistaken in the belief that net zero doesn't really apply to them. Neither viewpoint could be further from reality.

As we know, climate change is an emotive and controversial subject. There are many distractions and noises to contend with, including politics, jargon, popular opinion and headline-grabbing activities generated by the likes of flat earthers and superglue-wielding activists. This chapter, therefore, aims to get to the essence of what all this means as it relates to the cold, hard business case with both climate science and emotion removed.

And so, this is as good a place as any to understand the context that SMEs operate within so that we can all be ready to support them through this huge economic transition.

Context vs perception

In 2019, when the UK Government amended the Climate Change Act of 2008[2] it included its commitment to achieve net zero by 2050. In this respect, the UK was a pioneer, the first of the major global economies to legislate its target ambition of reaching 100% reduction.

---

2 27th June 2019

It couldn't have been clearer, except for the fact that the wider public awareness of the issues involved was less than encouraging.

In a 2021 survey carried out by the UK Government[3] of nearly 7,000 members of the public examining public awareness and perceptions of net zero, 87% of respondents confirmed they were aware of it. When asked, `What does net zero mean to you?' the results showed:

- 42% said this equated to `zero emissions.'
- 28% said it meant `reducing emissions to as low as possible'.
- 21% correctly identified it means balancing emissions with removals.

While there clearly was a gap in understanding the correct meaning of net zero, almost 80% believed it was an important enough target to support. *But what does that actually translate to in terms of action?* We don't truthfully know. Those in the 79th percentile may only be concerned enough to dabble with recycling, and that's it. Some in the 81st percentile may be diligent recyclers, but only because they're told they must, or their bins won't be emptied.

Answers to surveys linked to a series of fixed, multiple-choice questions don't tell us much about the real world, where opinion sits across a spectrum of thoughts and beliefs. It's a basis on which to build, nevertheless. On that basis, and Inspired by the *Pareto Principle*, I will assume (with some creative license) that the same broad 80:20 split exists amongst business owners from all walks of life when it comes to their own climate concerns and motivation to take action. As an

---

[3] UK Government, *Climate Change and Net Zero: Public Awareness and Perceptions (Research Paper No. 2021/034)*, April 2021

optimist, I like to believe that by proactively positioning the business case for action, there's no reason why we can't reach that remaining 20%, too. That includes the hard-line group who oppose net zero and actively argue against it. Personally, I'm thoroughly opposed to some of the crazy marginal rates of income tax that exist in our tax system, but that doesn't stop me from advising clients on how best to navigate them.

The reality is that we need regulations and frameworks to ensure that other teams also play by the same rules. Like it or not, climate action in a business context is competitive and can lead to advantages and disadvantages that need to be navigated. We can only do that if we have a common language. Therefore, the definitions need to be clear. Let me cut through the noise and unpack some of the familiar terms that aren't well understood.

Net zero

Net zero involves reducing greenhouse gas (GHG) emissions as much as possible and balancing the remainder via carbon removals. We'll explore this further in Chapter 2.

Carbon neutral

Put simply, this is balancing out emissions with offsets. A business might measure its GHG emissions (of its product, service or organisation) and purchase and retire an equivalent amount of carbon credits. It can then claim that its carbon impact has been offset and neutralised. Did you notice how it doesn't specify that emissions *reduction* has taken place? A business that claims to be carbon neutral may well have actually increased their emissions because they can simply buy their way out of it. Behind a carbon neutral claim can be anything from hugely laudable reduction efforts to outrageous greenwashing. For example, the UK Advertising Standards Authority challenged Shell's 2020 'Drive Carbon Neutral' campaign, stating that Shell's `basis of environmental claims must be clear. Unqualified claims could mislead if they omit significant information.'[4] This wasn't some new, green fuel. It was the same fuel, used in the same quantities but offset by carbon credits. We'll look at equivalence issues between carbon credits and carbon emissions shortly.

Thankfully, the regulatory net is tightening when such claims are made, but the confusion as to what they mean will likely persist for some time. The sooner this is dealt with, the better, since greenwashing (misleading claims making businesses seem more sustainable than they truly are) can influence consumers into purchasing choices that aren't aligned with their climate action intentions. Therefore, we must showcase to SMEs our own efforts to reach net zero with a good degree of transparency and integrity. This is exactly why we need to understand what the different terminology means; for example, claiming a 'carbon neutral' status is, as I've noted above, not something to boast about. For many people, it's a term they will have noticed, even if it's not part of their everyday language. However, knowing that such terms are problematic is important in order to avoid making an inadvertent (or even well-intended) claim that amounts to greenwashing. There lies a path towards reputational damage.

In fact, On January 17, 2024, the European Parliament adopted a directive to combat greenwashing and misleading product

---

[4] ASA, Complaint Ref: **G20-1049869 Shell UK Ltd, 7th June 2023**

information. This legislation bans the use of generic environmental claims—such as:

> *'...environmentally friendly', 'natural', 'biodegradable', 'climate neutral' or 'eco', without proof of recognised excellent environmental performance relevant to the claim.*[5]*'*

At the time of writing this book, it remains to be seen if similar legislation will be introduced into UK law beyond the long-standing Green Claims Code that Shell fell foul of. Nevertheless, such a ruling from our largest trading partner is still likely to impact British products and services since so many brands are global.

In summary, aiming to be carbon neutral isn't enough of an incentive to reduce your carbon emissions. In fact, you could *increase* your emissions and still be 'carbon neutral' because you can buy your way out of your emissions increase. Not many businesses will put that on their press release.

Carbon negative

Depending on who makes the claim, you can take your pick from one of two definitions. One version is not that dissimilar to Carbon Neutral. The only difference is that it relies on offsets *exceeding* calculated (or projected) emissions. It sounds like an impressive claim. The problem is that these measurements are never entirely accurate since they rely on estimates of future emissions. *What happens at the end of a product's useful life? Will it be recycled, head to landfill, or be incinerated?* The more conscientious businesses might even go as far

[5] European Parliament Press Release, *MEPs adopt new law banning greenwashing and misleading product information*, 17th January 2024

as employing a policy to, say, 'double-offset' on the basis that their measurements contain some soft emission estimates. Those extra offsets simply hedge against that inaccuracy. It makes me wonder what the point of Carbon Neutral is when such measurements will never be accurate enough to be exactly offset!

A more meaningful definition of Carbon Negative would be a business moving beyond carbon avoidance offsets and embedding carbon removal into their operations or products. Microsoft, who claimed to have been operationally carbon neutral since 2012, are to be fully carbon negative across both its operations and its supply chain by 2030. Their stated aim is a version of going beyond net zero;

`By 2030, Microsoft will be carbon negative, and by 2050, Microsoft will remove from the environment all the carbon the company has emitted either directly or by electrical consumption since it was founded in 1975.[6]'

To reach that goal, Microsoft laid out a roadmap that was as much about culture as it was about technology. They pledged to power all operations on 100% renewable energy by 2025, introduced an internal carbon fee so every division pays for its emissions, and set up a billion-dollar Climate Innovation Fund to accelerate the development of new carbon reduction and removal technologies. Fast-forward a few years and the explosion of energy-hungry AI has made that pledge harder to deliver, with their reported emissions rising as new data centres come

---

[6] Microsoft will be carbon negative by 2030 – https://blogs.microsoft.com/blog/2020/01/16/microsoft-will-be-carbon-negative-by-2030/

online. Yet Microsoft hasn't back-pedalled. Instead, they've doubled down, striking nuclear and carbon-free power agreements, expanding supplier requirements, and committing billions more to large-scale carbon removal contracts. AI has undeniably made the challenge harder, but the company continues to insist that the destination, being carbon negative by 2030, remains the same.

So when a company tells you it's carbon negative, you have to ask: what do they mean? Is it just a case of buying more avoidance credits and calling it progress, or is it a deeper shift into real reductions and carbon removal? Microsoft's stated aim sits in the latter camp to go beyond net zero and actively draw down the carbon they've put into the atmosphere since 1975. That distinction matters, because the gap between those two versions is the difference between a marketing claim and meaningful climate action.

Carbon Credits

To understand the concept of balancing out the emissions that can't be reduced within net zero, we need to understand some of the complexity around carbon credits. Carbon credits are a strange invention. They're permits or certificates that *allow* the owner to emit a certain amount of carbon dioxide or other greenhouse gases (collectively known as CO2e or carbon dioxide equivalent). Typically, one carbon credit equals one ton of CO2e. These carbon credits can be traded until they're used as an offset, at which point they are `retired'.

So, where do these emissions permissions originate? In general, they each have their roots in `projects'. Everything, from distributing solar-powered stoves to rural populations in Eritrea at a carbon credit price of around $5 per tonne of CO2e ***avoided***; rainforest protection emissions reduction projects similarly priced at around $10 per tonne of CO2e ***reduced***, and ultimately the Climeworks direct air capture and storage facility in Iceland (literally sucking carbon dioxide out of the air and shoving it deep underground to be mineralised) at around $1,000 per tonne of CO2e permanently ***removed***.

I've been using the words avoidance, reduction and removal to describe the ways in which a business would approach its offsetting. They each refer to a classification type. Or, to put it another way, how good the credit is, and how permanent it is. Ultimately, how close it is to an equivalence with simply leaving the fossil fuels in the ground – which is what we achieve through our own emissions reduction actions.

Carbon neutral claims merely need avoidance offsets. Net zero requires permanent removals. *Ouch!* There are cheaper options than Climeworks, but still.

To learn more about carbon credits, visit https://jameslizars.com/blog.

Carbon offsetting

If carbon credits are the mechanism, then carbon offsetting is the behaviour. And, let's be clear, carbon offsetting is deeply problematic. However, I also believe that we should do a version of it where we can. Allow me to explain.

The concept of carbon offsetting is quite simple. On the one hand, what you *produce* in one area, you reduce in another. The scales then even out, so job done: you're carbon neutral.

Except, as we now know, it's not that simple in reality. Probably the biggest issue is the question of equivalence. For example, if you take a short hop flight from London to Glasgow, chances are your airline will offer you the opportunity to avail yourself of its carbon offset scheme. That all seems worthwhile and positive – except you have to wonder whether the carbon emitted during that flight is equivalent to whatever offsetting project you've paid for. Perhaps that project states it protects a piece of land from deforestation (a popular example of offsetting projects; many are Gold Standard verified, which sounds impressive!). That carbon credit is retired forevermore, and no one else can buy it. *So, is it equivalent?*

And here is where we get into some of the technical difficulties with carbon offsets:

1) **Additionality** – is there *really* an additional impact? In 2015, 196 parties adopted the Paris Agreement as a legally binding international treaty on climate change. Is the 86 tonnes of CO2e avoidance offsets that my business has purchased under the Gold Standard Edirne Wind Energy project in Turkey *really* additional? Or might the Turkish government have decarbonised their energy supply anyway, as part of their 2053 net zero commitment?

2) **Permanence** - is the carbon reduction or removal genuinely permanent? Our business has made strong progress towards our million-tree pledge, but I'd be lying if I said I thought our coastal mangroves and inland plantations were safe from disease, forest fires and rising sea-levels.

3) **Leakage** – could avoiding emissions in one place push them to another place? Deforestation protection projects have geographical boundaries. What's preventing the urge to clear land from being shifted to the other side of those boundaries?

My point is carbon offsets don't work on a neat and tidy like-for-like basis. If you burn fossil fuel *today,* there's carbon in the air *today*. How many trees must a frequent flyer plant to offset their carbon footprint? How do we count the years those trees have been saplings?

Offsetting isn't some magic solution, it can only ever be a partial answer. Used wisely, it can complement direct reductions. Used carelessly, it risks becoming a distraction from the harder, more meaningful work of avoiding emissions in the first place.

Of course, I wouldn't suggest dismissing investments in carbon offset projects completely. It's important to support countries such as Turkey in *accelerating* their investment in renewables projects or in Africa, where solar stoves are distributed so people can stop burning solid fuels and reduce deforestation. These, and similar projects, are important projects with a diverse array of other benefits.

I worry that such investments are perceived to achieve the wrong purpose, and therefore, people don't do them: offsetting isn't the same as cancelling, but it is a **good** step to take. I'm proud to say that in my own business, we've paid a specialist subscription-based service provided by Ecologi[7] and have offset well over 300 tonnes of CO2e even though our annual emissions are 30 tonnes. This equates to a complete offset of our business lifetime emissions to date - for less than £1000! Engaging with Ecologi certainly opened our minds to understanding the options available and identifying the nuances and differences within the general terminology.

---

[7] Ecologi's stated mission is 'to inspire and empower businesses to accelerate global climate action'. For more information visit https://ecologi.com

"At Ecologi, we started with a simple idea: businesses of any size should have a meaningful way to take climate action without feeling overwhelmed. We are here to make that journey easier and more impactful, helping companies support real climate solutions while working hard to reduce their own emissions. It is all about progress, not perfection."

"We see carbon offsetting not as the destination, but as an important step alongside real reductions. By making a genuine climate contribution today, businesses can help drive the shift toward a net zero future. It is not about ticking a box. It is about showing leadership, inspiring others, and helping to build the kind of economy we all want to see."

Elliot Coad, Founder Ecologi

Let's not beat around the bush - using carbon credits to offset our business-as-usual emissions without taking the necessary steps to reduce those emissions directly will not solve climate change. Honestly, I've never used carbon neutrality as a claim because it just never felt enough. What I do claim, however, is that I've made a **climate contribution,** and I'm comfortable in that assertion because the more I've made an effort to learn what the various terminologies mean – and what the impacts of their actions represent in reality – then this allows me to speak to a level of expertise and depth of understanding beyond the norm.

This is my first challenge to you:

- Familiarise yourself with the basics so that you are also viewed as a trusted authority, especially in the eyes of your clients (I explain the importance of this in Chapter 3).

As small businesses, we should seek to influence others, and if we can build on this understanding and encourage more people to be on the front edge of education on this subject, then all the better. And believe me, it won't just be your clients that sit up and take notice – it will be those nearer to home in your business itself, especially those you seek to attract in the future.

Actions you can take will contribute to the 2050 net zero target. Knowing and understanding the terminology and then understanding where you can make the most impactful change will serve not only your business and your clients, but also, the planet.

CHAPTER 2

WHAT IS NET ZERO FOR BUSINESS?

In the previous chapter, I mentioned that the definition of the term net zero isn't as obvious as it sounds. To some, it can also feel like an abstract concept associated with big government and media-grabbing headlines. You might even think that it has little or nothing to do with your day-to-day SME's operations and that the best response is to `keep calm and carry on'.

The reality is that a `keep calm and carry on' attitude is no longer an option. Not if you want your business to thrive, survive and be sustainable in the evolving landscape of regulation. The drive to reach net zero means that the rules of doing business are changing, not just for the big corporates but for all of us. Someone, somewhere in our value chain, will have eyes on what it is we're doing to decarbonise, and that won't be because they're looking for us to become eco-warriors or climate activists. It's because regulatory requirements and compliance don't sit just at the top of the chain; they cascade throughout, and as SMEs, we're seen as both part of the problem and the solution.

In which case, have you been pledged to net zero by a customer? If so:

- Are you clear on what this means regarding your business output and commitment?
- If not, now is the time to consider what lies ahead.

Why? Because your big-ticket clients are on the hunt for data about where they're responsible for emissions, not just from within their own backyard but also from within their supply chain. That means you. In short, they'll want to determine exactly how your efforts will reduce their supply chain emissions, which means they'll look to you to achieve net zero.

My own business is a Tier 2 supplier, through a couple of our clients, to a major high street bank that's committed to net zero, and there are many similar links throughout our client base. As part of our clients' supply chain, we're also committed to net zero. Do we have credible plans for achieving it? Honestly? No, but we do have a target and have already demonstrated action. We also know what we're going to do next.

In this chapter, I'll explain the fuller definition of net zero and Scopes 1, 2, and 3, which offers a clearer understanding of how regulations apply to SMEs as well as the key sources of emissions that need to be tackled.

Not all net zeros are created equal.

Often, the first step of a net zero commitment is to set a target. Not just any target, but an **ambitious** target. And how will you know if you've set the right path in order to reach it? In fact, what exactly does net zero mean again?

Finding the answer to that question is not such an easy task. Perhaps you've already found yourself at the bottom of the rabbit hole following a `what is net zero?' search via Google. If so, I bet you've eye-rolled at the return results - an endless list of corporates and big businesses: worthy statements, case studies, reports and objectives. Click through any, and you get their why (crisis), their what (achievements) and their how (strategic plan) as they scramble towards the 2050 net zero goal.

In 2023, just under half of the Forbes Global 2000 companies, around 50% by count, covering two-thirds of total revenue, had set net-zero targets. Yet only 4% of those had plans that met credible international standards. By 2024, the number of companies with net-zero targets had risen to about 60%, again representing roughly two-thirds of revenue. But the proportion with robust, integrity-based plans barely moved, edging up to only 5%. This shows two truths at once: the momentum of corporate commitments is growing, but credibility still lags badly. And importantly, this uptick is happening despite shifting political winds, a signal that net zero is being driven less by partisan policy and more by the demands of global markets, investors, and supply chains.

From an SME's perspective, little of this information overload seems relatable. Except that, almost certainly, your business **will** be somebody else's Scope 3, indirect emissions. If they're committed to net zero, so must you be. This is a core element of the business case. The question is, *Where do you start?* Followed immediately by *How much can you net off to achieve zero?*

Reducing emissions by 5% and netting the remainder with rainforest protection offsets won't be adequate. However, we can all approach this by reducing emissions as much as possible and working towards balancing the remainder with offsets. The problem SMEs face is that not all net zero targets are equal, and there is no single global standard to define what we must do. Also, no two businesses are the same, so, `As much as possible' means different things to different businesses. No wonder it can be confusing, especially since a whole host of voluntary global standards have arisen over time, setting definitions for net zero that depend on various factors.

For example, take the United Nations *Race to Zero* initiative. It invites SMEs to join the race by visiting the dedicated SME Climate Hub[8], which offers valuable resources. The aim is to help SMEs estimate their full carbon footprint and `find quick-win actions to reduce emissions.' Or you can choose to follow the guidelines as set out by ISO (the International Organisation for Standardisation)[9] which offers a set of `guiding principles and recommendations to enable a common, global approach to achieving net zero GHG emissions through alignment of voluntary initiatives and adoption of standards, policies that include both national and international regulation.'[10] Once again, all very

[8] https://smeclimatehub.org/
[9] https://www.iso.org/net zero
[10] ISO, IWA 42:2022(en) Net zero guidelines, Chapter 1 – Scope

https://www.iso.org/obp/ui/en/#iso:std:iso:iwa:42:ed-1:v1:en

laudable and a welcome addition, but note the word 'voluntary' in its opening chapter.

Nearer to home, there's the business sector roadmap[11] published by the UK Government's *Net Zero Council* to help guide the development of robust and consistent roadmaps. Whilst they're not all completely identical, there has been collaboration and a strong convergence, but what's common is their alignment with the 1.5-degree goal adopted by 196 countries at COP21 (known as the Paris Agreement) in November 2015. Several countries (including the UK) have legislated for net zero whilst others have pledged, a pattern mirrored by businesses. However, in a step forward, shortly after the COP27 gathering in Egypt in November 2022, the SBTi (Science Based Targets Initiative) finalised its definition of net zero[12], and this is the closest to a common framework that most corporate bodies seem to have adopted and is probably the most visible to business leaders. It states that corporate and global businesses should aim for a 90% reduction of emissions across all scopes with a target 50% reduction by 2030. The point of difference for SMEs is they need to achieve 90% across Scopes 1 and 2. However, there is no specific target to reduce across Scope 3, only a commitment to do so.

Evidently, not all net zeros are the same. While some businesses have made a substantial SBTi-aligned commitment to net zero (with a few on accelerated timeframes), some are nowhere near this. Of those that have committed, only a tiny fraction have robust plans for achieving their targets simply because it's not easy to accurately predict what

[11] https://www.gov.uk/government/publications/net -zero-business-sector-roadmap-guidelines
[12] https://sciencebasedtargets.org/resources/files/Net -Zero-Standard.pdf

comes next. In which case, what chances do we as SMEs have of both making a start on our plans and achieving them?

- Firstly, we need to acknowledge that net zero can't be ignored.
- Secondly, it's essential to commit to making a plan.

Unpicking the jargon (see Chapter 1) is key so that you're better informed about what you should aim for and how to determine where your business is generating emissions. In short, any of your business's activities will create emissions. Any part of its operations, its existence, and the way it interfaces with the world, the economy, customers and employees generates some kind of emission, some of it is direct, much of it indirect.

Where your emissions come from

Greenhouse Gases (GHGs) absorb heat radiated from the Earth's surface and atmosphere, re-emitting it and trapping warmth. This regulates Earth's temperature but, when intensified by human emissions, leads to global warming. This is the greenhouse effect. The main villain most people talk about is Carbon Dioxide (CO_2), but there are five more GHGs we should keep in our sights to achieve a net zero ambition.

- CO_2 – Carbon dioxide emissions are the primary driver of global climate change.
- CH_4 - Methane enters the atmosphere via human-related activities and natural sources, particularly livestock. 70% of emissions are linked to human-related activities.

- NO_2 - Nitrogen dioxide is primarily released from burning fuel in cars, buses and lorries.
- HFCs – Hydrofluorocarbons are a collection of man-made gases with global warming potentials many times that of carbon dioxide. They are used as coolants in fridges and air conditioning units.
- PFCs – Perfluorocarbons are also man-made and typically used within the electronic industry to produce semiconductors, without which we'd have no smartphones, TVs, computers, or advanced medical diagnostic equipment.
- SF6 - Sulphur hexafluoride – Another synthetic gas that's even more potent than CO2, and is mostly used today within the electricity industry so that we can keep the lights on and our computers running.

Fig 1. Scopes 1, 2 & 3 emission sources

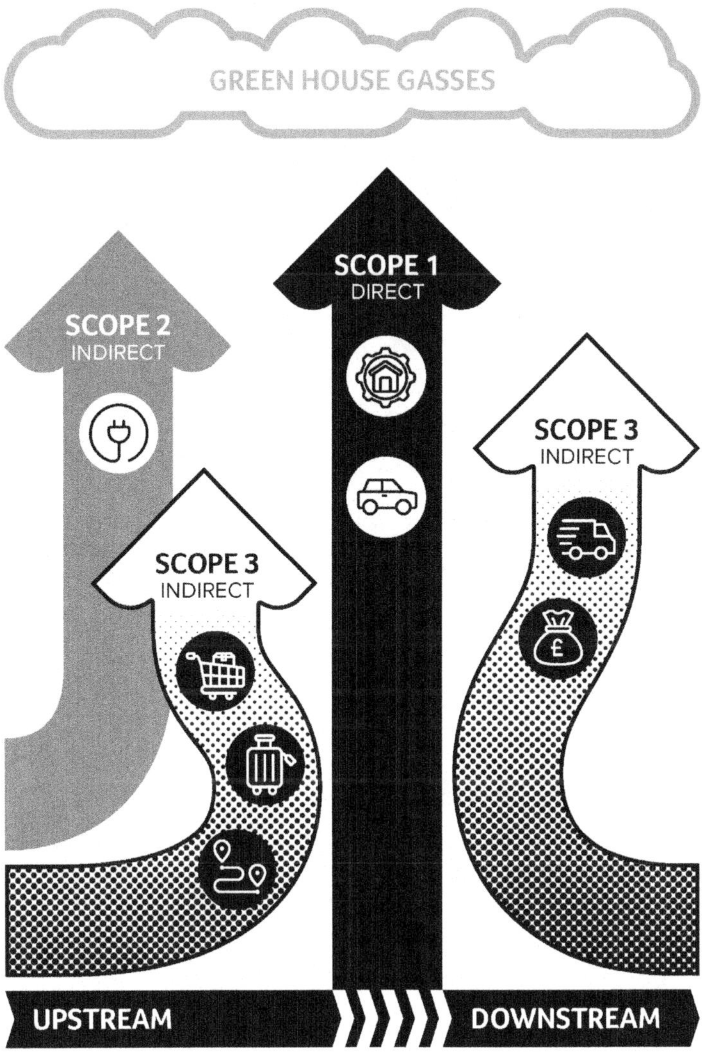

- **Scope 1** - These are GHG emissions that your business makes directly, where it's burning fossil fuels such as petrol, diesel, methane, etc.

- **Scope 2** - These are indirect emissions due to the energy that's not necessarily renewable, produced by third parties that burn fossil fuels on your behalf. The business then buys in the energy produced (electricity to heat/cool and light its buildings).
- **Scope 3** – This is the most complex area to measure since these are emissions not directly produced by the business itself but by customers and suppliers within its value chain, including the use and disposal of products.

Scope 1

In many respects, how you tackle Scope 1 is the easiest to grapple with because it generally relies on efficiency gains or capital investment decisions (some more significant than others) and reorganising areas of operational logistics that currently directly impact emissions. Such as:

- Can you switch from diesel/petrol and electrify some or all of your vehicle fleet?
- Can gas boilers be replaced with heat pumps?
- What energy efficiency measures can be taken?

Identifying and quantifying the sources of emissions and then examining reduction options becomes a more familiar game of numbers laid out on a spreadsheet.

- Do the options present a real investment case in their own right?
- Will such an investment save the business money in the long run?
- Will your actions reduce your emissions in line with your target?

Big issues, big questions, and possibly significant financial commitments are involved. But we're accountants, right? This is what we do: we analyse the data, scrutinise it and apply our knowledge and expertise to identify those necessary insights that inform the decision-making of any business, large or small. Assuming the business isn't part of the blast furnace sector, your solution may be a heat pump since they're more energy efficient and can operate on renewable energy. And here's a thought: *Maybe that will save money too!* With plenty of grants and tax incentives, could the payback period be surprisingly short?

Honestly, it's no easy task to decarbonise a business heavy on Scope 1. In 2023, British Steel announced its proposal to replace its heavy coal-fired, carbon-emitting furnaces with electric arc steelmaking (EAF) as part of its ambition to reduce its CO_2 emissions by 75%. Without a doubt, that's a huge decision, especially as it was projected to result in up to 2,500 job losses. On a more positive note, for car manufacturers that rely on steel production, this transition from coal-fired steel to green hydrogen is something they can shout about as part of their green credentials. For example, Volvo collaborated with Swedish steel maker SSAB to jointly explore the development of fossil-free, high-quality steel for use in the automotive industry. Volvo announced that the `result is expected to be the world's first fossil-free steelmaking technology, with virtually no carbon footprint.'[13]

That's a big claim, but it highlights how we aren't dependent on as-yet-undiscovered technologies of the future. Improving upon and scaling

[13] Volvo press release, ID 282789, 16th June, 2021 https://www.media.volvocars.com/global/en-gb/media/pressreleases/282789/volvo-cars-is-first-car-maker-to-explore-fossil-free-steel-with-ssab

existing technologies is the near-term pathway. Considering the global steel industry is responsible for 7%[14] of CO_2 emissions, even such carbon-belching, heavy industries are finding an investment case to decarbonise.

Scope 2

Simply put, the fossil fuels that someone else burns for you.

The most obvious example is purchased electricity, so you might believe that switching to a renewable tariff is your bit done concerning managing Scope 2.

Except it's not quite that simple because, in reality, all that effectively achieves is more fossil fuels used by someone else instead. In fact, your decision-making process may well lay in where your physical location is due to renewable energy availability that varies by region:

- Southeast England = 25%.
- Scotland = 80%.

If you're wondering why, Scotland is typically windier and can draw energy from its higher proportion of wind turbines. This accounts for this part of the UK achieving 97%[15] of its net zero targets compared to 32%[16] as measured across the whole of the UK.

---

[14] International Energy Agency report, *Iron and Steel Technology Roadmap: Towards more sustainable steelmaking*, October 2022

[15] https://www.scottishrenewables.com/our-industry/statistics

[16] ONS, *Climate change insights, families and households UK*, August 2023 - https://www.ons.gov.uk/economy/environmentalaccounts/articles/climatechangeinsightsuk/august2023

It's confusing because Scope 2 isn't in your direct control - not really if you take some time to do some homework. The solution will invariably boil down to a conscious investment decision that will deliver long-term results to the business.

For example, if you own premises operating generally between 9 am - 5 pm, consider investing and installing solar panels. Alternatively, the UK is seeing a rise in cooperative generation schemes where a business can purchase shares in renewable generation projects[17] (solar and wind power) that feed that energy back to the business via their energy supplier. This is particularly beneficial if you move premises as you can still retain access to your renewable supply. Either option not only reduces your reliance on volatile energy markets but also makes a significant contribution towards your own net zero goals. As we collectively progress through the decarbonisation of the National Grid, your Scope 2 emissions will naturally reduce.

Or you could choose a renewable tariff[18] where the profits are ploughed back into demonstrably renewable projects. I'm not pretending that switching to a renewable tariff is **the** answer, but it will be a significant switch. And it's part of the story your business can tell in its net zero narrative. It will also be noted within your supply chain. And, economics 1.01, more solutions will be provided as demand increases for similar schemes.

Be part of that demand – and, therefore, the solution.

---

[17] Octopus Energy is a leading renewable energy supplier that has taken the UK lead https://octopus.energy/blog/community-energy/

[18] For a quick comparison of renewable green energy suppliers visit https://www.energyhelpline.com/

There's no need to let the jargon and noise surrounding net zero, or the resultant fear of green investment prevent you from taking positive steps towards managing your Scope 2.

The UK energy regulator, Ofgem, has created a free online guide to `help you find small business energy grants, schemes and advice to lower your carbon emissions and get more efficient with your commercial energy use'. [19]

Scope 3

This is the big one that causes quite a few headaches in the boardroom. *Why?* Because it's where SMEs are part of their bigger corporate client's supply chain net zero ambitions. And that can feel like a power imbalance.

For example, in the years since the Paris Agreement, Barclays Bank has been one of the largest investors in fossil fuel projects, even if they're not the ones actually drilling for gas and oil or mining for coal. And yet, in their Annual Reports, they've claimed to be aligned to SBTi standards that will see emissions reduced by 50% by 2030 and to 90% by 2050. Additionally, Barclays also state that their most significant source of emissions (80%) emanates from Scope 3 – which, in this case, means mainly from within their suppliers and customers. In short, that means issuing contracts only with suppliers with their own net zero targets and plans in place.

[19] guide will help you find small business energy grants, schemes and advice to lower your carbon emissions and get more efficient with your commercial energy use.

The big corporates are compelled to reduce their Scope 3 emissions by 90% according to the SBTi framework; SMEs are only expected to commit to a reduction that can then be demonstrably verified. These may be relatively simple changes, such as swapping domestic flights for train travel and purchasing refurbished IT kit rather than new. Or it may be pursuing the much tougher challenge of engaging with suppliers who may be significantly larger than them.

Summary

As accountants, we're already well-equipped to identify business emissions. Our expertise in rules-based frameworks helps us apply them naturally to a business. We instinctively understand how changes impact the P&L and how to support decision-making through the insights we gain from our deep knowledge of a business.

Who knew that sustainability expertise wasn't essential when a spreadsheet can reveal so much? How we analyse numbers begins to tell its own story, where emissions are created and, crucially, how to reduce them. The data suggests solutions, which we evaluate through a commercial lens to justify action. Managing Scope 3 isn't about climate science; it's about understanding the net zero framework and making informed decisions on emissions driven by business activity.

Even though Scope 3 emissions are indirect, they form the most significant weighting. They cover upstream activities such as the goods and services you buy in, employee commuting, and home working, as well as downstream activities such as product usage, distribution and waste. Which covers pretty much everything peripheral in the business ecosystem. Or to put it another way, wherever there's an expenditure, there's almost always an emission.

Nor does it stop there. Businesses are under increasing scrutiny as to where they then deposit their revenues: perhaps that's with a financial institution better known for funding fossil fuel projects (Barclays[20]) or an altogether `greener' outfit (Starling Bank[21]) that refuses to lend to fossil fuel producers and has developed an integrated carbon reduction plan that underpins its business operations.

Here's what we need to remind ourselves of: **every** business, to a greater or lesser degree, emits GHGs, including yours and mine. Even though my own is a straightforward B2B service provider, once we began to strip away the areas of physical product generation that don't apply to it, we still found it ticked many of the emission boxes. That was a real eye-opener, considering ourselves as a low-carbon emitter. It shouldn't have been a real surprise because whenever a business employs people, they must be provided with electricity and heat, whether on-site or working from home.

---

[20] Significantly, in February 2024 Barclays announced that it would no longer provide direct funding for new oil and gas projects.
[21] Starling Bank's carbon reduction plan https://www.starlingbank.com/about/carbon-reduction-plan/

CHAPTER 3

REGULATION

The Path from ESG to Regulation

Environmental, Social and Governance (ESG), has grown in popularity over recent years, amongst finance professionals at least. But there's surprisingly little understanding of its origins and purpose. ESG has become an all-encompassing term, similar to `sustainability', and has become shorthand for describing doing good in business. A progression from CSR (Corporate Social Responsibility), perhaps. Businesses, investors, and even regulatory bodies use it in varied ways, creating a disconnect between perception and reality.

At Thrive, as a B Corp, we use the B Impact Assessment[22] framework to drive continuous improvement across the pillars of People, Planet,

---

[22] https://www.bcorporation.net/en-us/programs-and-tools/b-impact-assessment/

and Profit. Our commitment extends beyond box-ticking, generating an increasingly positive impact across all stakeholder groups, including the environment. Our B Corp score is one of the KPIs (key performance indicator) on our balanced scorecard, alongside MRR Growth (monthly recurring revenue), Profitability, Team Happiness and Client Net Promoter Score. We use the scorecard to track our progress and the B Impact Assessment to highlight where we can do better. And we routinely push beyond conventional business practices to try more progressive ways of doing things with different, positive impacts on stakeholders.

We've taken numerous steps to reduce our GHG emissions. We commit 20% of our profits to nature restoration projects, and our small team has funded planting more than 300,000 trees as of 2025[23]. Our recruitment process includes redacted CV screening to remove indicators of race, gender, and socio-economic background. Despite me being the sole director, we also have monthly board meetings. These efforts, amongst many other initiatives and policies, have brought commercial successes such as dream clients seeking us out, attracting and retaining fantastic team members and a growth rate that I wouldn't want to be higher for the impact it would have on my family life. We are a ***good*** business in the modern sense. We also attained national industry recognition as the ESG (small firms) category winner at the 2024 Accounting Excellence Awards.

Yet, this presents something of an oddity. Winning an ESG award for our impact has little alignment with what ESG originally measures in investment or regulatory contexts. Initially conceived as an investment risk framework, ESG assesses a company's financial vulnerability to

---

[23] https://www.veritree.com/impact-hub/thrive

climate, governance, and social risks rather than its proactive contributions to sustainability. This explains why ExxonMobil can rank highly on ESG indexes while companies like Tesla may be excluded.

Elon Musk, famously disruptive in industries before crossing over to politics, labelled ESG `an outrageous scam[24]' after Tesla was excluded from the S&P 500 ESG ranking[25], despite ExxonMobil retaining its place. Tesla's omission seemed illogical, even for staunch climate denialists, given its focus on electric transport. Tesla's exclusion was not due to environmental shortcomings but to deficiencies in social and governance areas, including accusations of poor working conditions and governance weaknesses. Conversely, ExxonMobil maintained strong governance structures and detailed climate risk disclosures, making it a safer investment according to ESG criteria.

This distinction matters. As financial markets increasingly depended on ESG metrics, investors sought clearer, standardised sustainability reporting frameworks. So, voluntary frameworks like the Task Force on Climate-related Financial Disclosures (TCFD) emerged, setting the stage for mandatory reporting standards.

Interestingly, net zero isn't explicitly mandated within current regulations. Instead, regulations focus on setting clear standards, reporting requirements, and accountability frameworks businesses must follow to demonstrate credible progress towards net zero.

---

[24] Elon Musk, *X.com* (formerly known as Twitter*),* 18 May, 2022

[25] The S&P 500 ESG Index (Dow Jones) is a broad-based, market-cap-weighted index designed to measure the performance of securities meeting sustainability criteria, while maintaining similar overall industry group weights as the S&P 500.

Historically, climate risk disclosure was voluntary, guided by frameworks like TCFD and the Science-Based Targets Initiative (SBTi). Now, voluntary disclosures are evolving into mandatory requirements. The International Sustainability Standards Board (ISSB) introduced IFRS S1 & S2 standards[26], anticipated to become the global baseline for climate-related financial disclosures, promoting consistency across industries.

What Does IFRS S1 & S2 Mean Practically?

IFRS S1 is a general standard for sustainability reporting, requiring disclosures of sustainability-related risks and opportunities that could impact a business's financial outcomes.

IFRS S2 specifically addresses climate-related disclosures, outlining the need for detailed information on governance, strategy, risk management, and metrics and targets related to climate risks and opportunities.

Should SMEs voluntarily align with these standards? Voluntary alignment with IFRS S1 & S2 could help SMEs build trust with investors, partners, and customers. It may also proactively prepare them for inevitable regulatory shifts and new market demands, strategically positioning them for future opportunities.

The UK's stance contrasts with the EU's broader Corporate Sustainability Reporting Directive (CSRD) framework. Currently, the UK aligns with ISSB's single materiality approach, focusing primarily on how climate risks financially affect businesses. Single materiality emphasises assessing the financial impact climate issues have on an

---

[26] https://www.ifrs.org/sustainability/tcfd/

organisation rather than how the organisation affects the broader environment and society.

ESG has historically only pointed inwards. Looking at how ESG factors impact the business.

In contrast, the EU's CSRD employs double materiality, requiring companies to report not only on financial risks but also their impact on society and the environment. This approach significantly broadens the scope of disclosures, encompassing areas like biodiversity, social justice, and broader governance issues.

So, why does this distinction matter practically? SMEs in the UK might initially consider double materiality an EU-only issue. And even then, just for the largest businesses (for now). However, it signals an inevitable global regulatory direction, likely influencing UK regulation. Carbon import levies, such as the EU's Carbon Border Adjustment Mechanism (CBAM)[27], further emphasise the importance of proactively preparing for broader disclosure requirements.

The Ripple Effect: Indirect Regulatory Pressures

Even SMEs not directly mandated by climate regulations encounter indirect pressures from stakeholders, including customers, banks, insurers, landlords, and investors. These pressures increasingly influence business decisions.

For instance, banks frequently integrate ESG criteria into lending decisions, insurers evaluate climate risk in underwriting, and

[27] Carbon Border Adjustment Mechanism (CBAM) for goods that are entering the EU https://taxation-customs.ec.europa.eu/carbon-border-adjustment-mechanism_en

commercial landlords are factoring ESG considerations into lease agreements. SMEs without clear sustainability credentials may soon face higher costs or financial or insurance restrictions.

Public procurement is another powerful indirect regulatory driver. Procurement Policy Note (PPN) 006 mandates suppliers bidding for government contracts above £5 million annually to provide credible carbon reduction plans covering Scope 1, 2, and select Scope 3 emissions and a 2050 net zero target. However, given the NHS's influential approach, applying these criteria irrespective of financial thresholds, the £5 million threshold will likely soon decrease.

NHS Evergreen Supplier Assessment

The NHS Evergreen Supplier Assessment is a sophisticated procurement evaluation tool developed by NHS England to assess suppliers' sustainability credentials. Suppliers are categorised based on their demonstrated commitment to sustainability across several key areas:

Category	**Requirements**
Carbon Reduction	Suppliers must set and report clear, science-based targets aligned with the NHS's net zero goals.
Resource Efficiency	Demonstrable waste reduction, sustainable resource management, and circular economy initiatives.
Social Value	Commitment to fair labour practices, community benefits, and employee wellbeing.

Category	Requirements
Governance	Transparent sustainability governance structures, regular public disclosures of progress, and clear internal accountability processes.

This structured assessment influences procurement decisions, prioritising suppliers who perform strongly across these sustainability metrics. For SMEs, proactively meeting these expectations can unlock significant competitive advantages, securing long-term partnerships and lucrative NHS contracts.

Professional Competence and the Accountant's Role

As accountants, we complete Continuing Professional Development (CPD) annually, affirming our ongoing duty to maintain professional competence. In today's environment, sustainability is a critical component of that competence. Suppose we neglect to keep abreast of sustainability reporting frameworks, regulatory developments, emerging risks, and the significant business opportunities these present, or worse, consider them beyond our professional scope; we risk failing our fundamental duty to clients and employers alike.

Professional competence in accounting now requires more than technical financial expertise. It demands awareness of evolving sustainability standards, climate-related disclosures, and changing stakeholder ESG expectations. Staying updated isn't simply about compliance; but delivering timely, relevant, and strategic advice. Professional bodies like ACCA proactively address this by offering specialised resources such as ACCA's Professional Diploma in Sustainability[28]. Such programmes ensure accountants remain professionally relevant, prepared for current requirements and strategically positioned for future developments.

You may be wondering why I'm raising this point about professional competence. Earlier, I asked, `When do we ever get such foresight of a major shift in the business context?'. This is why. We're forewarned, and it would be pragmatic to be forearmed.

Discounting Future Climate Risks: A Financial Blind Spot

With this long-term thinking in mind, let's look at traditional financial valuation methods, particularly discounted cash flow (DCF) analysis, which often underestimates climate risks by heavily discounting their future impacts. DCF inherently favours short-term financial gains, making fossil-fuel-based investments appear more attractive initially if they present lower upfront costs. This approach has historically been effective, but it's increasingly out of step with the realities of climate risk and the economic transition we're facing. *Why does this matter now?*

As accountants, we've typically relied on DCF for good reason - it's reliable, proven, and straightforward. But, given our clear foresight of accelerating economic transitions and physical climate risks, relying solely on traditional financial metrics is becoming increasingly risky. Imagine an SME investing today in cheaper fossil-fuel-powered machinery based purely on short-term cost savings. *What happens*

---

[28] https://www.accaglobal.com/uk/en/qualifications/glance/professional-diploma-in-sustainability/overview.html

when carbon pricing escalates, regulations tighten, or market preferences swiftly shift towards lower-carbon solutions? Suddenly, that seemingly prudent financial decision becomes costly and strategically problematic.

Instead, accountants must blend rigorous financial analysis with informed professional judgment. We must proactively guide our businesses toward future-proof decisions that might initially look less attractive on paper but are far more financially prudent in the long run - recognising that this shift is crucial, not as an abstract theoretical exercise, but as an essential part of safeguarding the financial sustainability of SMEs.

Acting Now for Future Success

While SMEs may currently face indirect rather than direct regulatory mandates, the evolving landscape, including procurement expectations, investor scrutiny, and market-driven sustainability demands, makes proactive action essential. Accountants have an opportunity and responsibility to guide SMEs through this transition, turning regulatory challenges into clear strategic opportunities.

In Chapter 4, we'll explore attractive, commercially beneficial steps SMEs can adopt immediately, demonstrating how significant emissions reductions, including the crucial first milestone of a 50% reduction by 2030, are both achievable and economically advantageous. Sustainability isn't merely compliance; it's a strategic imperative for SMEs looking to thrive in a changing marketplace.

CHAPTER 4

BUSINESS DECISIONS THAT DON'T COST THE EARTH

Net zero isn't merely a reaction to the climate crisis; it's a robust concept in its own right and one that SMEs can and should respond to proactively. While the previous chapter explored how regulation shapes the landscape, this chapter will highlight the practical business cases and commercial opportunities net zero provides.

First, let's tackle a quick mindset shift. We're all accustomed to the familiar narrative around reducing carbon emissions, usually centred on personal lifestyle sacrifices:

- Go vegan!
- Drive electric!
- Stop flying!

- Give up your vehicle entirely!

While personal lifestyle changes are indeed important, they're beyond the direct scope of this book. Our focus here is on business decisions. It's natural to pause and ask, `What's actually in it for my business?' Personal sacrifices rarely frame business decision-making. Instead, commercial viability is the lens through which SMEs naturally evaluate their options.

Frequent portrayals of climate disasters, forest fires, floods, and hurricanes often seem distant from day-to-day business realities, creating disconnection rather than urgency. Yet, consider how SMEs are directly affected when climate events disrupt supply chains or cause unexpected spikes in raw material costs. While some actions have been taken, they're insufficient, particularly within the business community, where responses remain fragmented. What's crucial here is that we, as accountants, are uniquely placed to help our clients and business leaders look beyond the sensational headlines and overwhelming noise around net zero. By doing so, we enable clearer, more strategic decisions.

Using our strengths as accountants, curiosity, professional scepticism, analytical skills, data literacy, and the ability to interpret information and present insights, SMEs can seize clear commercial benefits from net zero through several key areas aligned with our professional expertise. These aren't about sacrifice; they're opportunities for resilience, competitive advantage, and long-term profitability.

1. Cost-saving

Reducing emissions often means lowering costs and vice versa. Here's a deeper dive into several practical actions SMEs can adopt, along with responses to potential objections you may face:

- **Refurbished IT Equipment:** Buying high-spec, refurbished IT equipment significantly lowers emissions and costs compared to new devices. At Thrive, we source our computers and electronics from Klyk[29], gaining quality equipment at a fraction of the cost.
    - *Objection:* `Isn't refurbished equipment risky?'
    - *Response:* `Trusted suppliers provide warranties and reliable equipment. At Thrive, partnering with Klyk ensures we achieve financial and net zero goals.'
- **Travel Policy:** Reducing air travel significantly cuts emissions and business costs. Particularly, limiting domestic flights can save substantially. Video conferencing often meets business needs effectively.
    - *Objection:* `Aren't trains often slower, pricier, or unreliable?'
    - *Response:* `Fair point. Trains can be pricey and occasionally unreliable. But consider hidden flight-related costs like taxis, parking, and lost productivity. Often, trains offer overall better value.'
- **Energy Efficiency:** Investing in energy-saving measures like LED lighting, smart plugs, motion detectors, and insulation, significantly reduces energy bills and emissions.
    - *Objection:* `Isn't the upfront cost a barrier?'

[29] Sustainable & Secure IT Built for Growth https://helloklyk.com/

    - *Response:* 'Grants, tax relief, and green financing can dramatically reduce initial costs. Often, payback periods are shorter than expected.'

- **Major Capital Expenditure:** Investments in big-ticket items like solar panels, heat pumps, efficient machinery, often deliver long-term savings and emissions reductions.
    - *Objection:* 'The upfront costs seem too high.'
    - *Response:* 'Grants and green financing can make these investments affordable. Payback periods can be surprisingly short, good ethics aligning with great business.'

Other ideas include greener procurement, digitalisation, sustainable packaging, vehicle fleet optimisation, and waste reduction.

The list goes on. Visit https://jameslizars.com/blog for more.

2. Access to supply chains

Chapter 3 addressed how SMEs risk losing supply chain access if they don't align with net zero commitments, the 'stick'. But let's now look at the 'carrot': the positive opportunities from proactive engagement.

Businesses that proactively embrace net zero stand out. Red Inc.[30], a Sussex-based stationery supplier, disrupted the national stationery market by demonstrating internal carbon reductions and proactively sourcing products aligned with PwC's net zero objectives. Red Inc. strategically aligned their offering to PwC's needs, winning substantial contracts over established competitors.

[30] Leading the way in sustainable office supplies solutions https://www.red-inc.com/

Barclays is Europe's largest financier of fossil fuel projects, yet (even) they are prioritising net zero within their supply chain. This approach illustrates clearly that proactive net zero alignment isn't merely ethical, it's commercially smart.

- **Objection:** `Won't aligning products and processes add complexity and cost?'
- **Response:** `Initially, yes. However, proactive alignment not only protects current contracts but also sets your SME apart. Red Inc. shows how surpassing net zero expectations can help SMEs compete successfully.'

This naturally leads us to consider going beyond simply positioning existing products or services as net zero-friendly towards exploring entirely new offerings specifically designed for net zero markets.

3. New revenue streams

Accountants can play a key role by identifying new business opportunities arising from net zero shifts.

Take promotional merchandise. Businesses are moving away from traditional leather-bound notebooks towards sustainably-produced alternatives. Moleskine, for instance, now offers vegan notebooks from FSC-certified forests. Platforms like Vinted, thriving on clothing resale, highlight consumer enthusiasm for reuse.

Brands like Elvis & Kresse, which makes luxury handbags from reclaimed fire hoses, and Nike's Space Hippie footwear, created from manufacturing scraps, illustrate successful commercial innovation around net zero.

> *'an exploratory footwear collection inspired by life on Mars—where materials are scarce, and there is no resupply mission. Created from scraps, or 'space junk', Space Hippie is the result of sustainable practices meeting radical design.'*[31]

According to Forbes, the Space Hippie collection has the lowest carbon footprint of any Nike footwear ever made.[32]

Yet Clayton Christensen's 'Innovator's Dilemma' warns of the risks of resisting innovation. Despite inventing the technology, Kodak famously hesitated to shift from profitable camera film to digital cameras, despite inventing that new technology. Fearful of disrupting their core business, they overlooked market shifts and ultimately went bankrupt. Kodak's story shows SMEs must actively embrace net zero opportunities to stay relevant and profitable.

Reputation

Every business taking net zero steps benefits from sharing its journey. Reputation matters significantly to customers, employees, and investors.

Customers:

Consumer research indicates that 62% of Gen Z prefer sustainable brands, and 73% of those will pay a premium for them[33]. This demonstrates clear customer-driven incentives to adopt net zero practices. The same principle applies in B2B contexts, where client

---

[31] https://www.nike.com/gb/space-hippie

[32] Blake Morgan, *How Companies Are Turning Trash Into Products (And Profits)*, Forbes (Online) 21 September. 2021

[33] First Insight (Whitepaper) *The State of Consumer Spending: Gen Z Shoppers Demand Sustainable Retail*, 14 January 2020

loyalty and long-term contracts increasingly depend on credible net zero credentials.

Employees:

Even during economic uncertainty, job seekers consider a company's environmental stance. KPMG research shows one-third of UK young people reject job offers based on poor sustainability records[34], underscoring the need for clear net zero actions. This emphasis extends to the retention and engagement of existing workers.

Investors:

Investors increasingly link sustainability with long-term returns. Larry Fink, CEO of BlackRock, initially declared,

> *'Climate risk is investment risk.'*

Four years later, he reported that sustainable investment had reached $4trn. But what was more illuminating was his statement that:

> *'We focus on sustainability not because we're environmentalists but because we are capitalists and fiduciaries to our clients.'*[35]

However, he recently clarified his focus on fiduciary responsibilities due to political pressures. Yet, his underlying point remains: sustainability is vital for investor confidence.

Actuaries are the masters of the long-term, using data, judgement, and foresight to turn uncertainty into opportunity, like putting a value today on pensions that will not be paid for 40 years. They echo the

---

[34] KMPG, *Climate quitting - younger workers voting with their feet on employer's ESG commitments*, 24 January 2023

[35] Larry Fink's letter to CEOs 2022, www.blackrock.com

sentiment with the Institute and Faculty of Actuaries' report, `The Emperor's New Climate Scenarios,'[36] which emphasises that climate risks are widely underestimated, underscoring the reputational and financial urgency for proactive net zero action.

Summary

We've made a strong case for SMEs embracing net zero as a strategic choice. But here's the key question: Who can best guide SMEs through this critical transition? Chapter 5 will explore why accountants are uniquely positioned to partner with SMEs on their net zero journey. Why, in fact, we are the catalyst that can transform net zero ambition into tangible, sustainable business success.

---

36 https://actuaries.org.uk/emperors-new-climate-scenarios

CHAPTER 5

PERSPECTIVE

I think you're awesome! No, really, I do!

With your inherent strengths, curiosity, analytical rigour, strategic insight, and professional scepticism, you already have the skills needed to help SMEs successfully navigate their net zero journeys. Your ability to interpret complex data, assess financial impacts, and provide clear, actionable insights positions you uniquely to ensure SMEs remain relevant and resilient in the face of current and future challenges. If this sounds ambitious, stick with me. I promise it's much closer to your day-to-day work than it might seem.

Perhaps you're thinking, *But isn't this all beyond what accountants usually do?* Actually, it's exactly what accountants are already perfectly equipped to handle. We have hidden superpowers that naturally align with tackling the net zero challenge. It doesn't need to mean a massive overhaul of your role, just a slight shift in perspective.

But let's pause for a moment. I can already imagine someone thinking, *Surely this is something for the big firms with ESG departments, not SMEs?* And yes, SMEs typically don't have specialist sustainability teams or extensive resources to dedicate to this. But that's precisely the point: SMEs have accountants. And accountants have what's needed to bridge that gap.

The benefits we bring

Our core proposition is built on trust, whether as in-house or external accountants. We've worked diligently to earn professional qualifications, demonstrating certified competency and integrity. Governed by rigorous ethical standards and professional oversight, we consistently maintain high levels of trust.

We naturally excel at interrogating complex and conflicting data. It's second nature for us to be curious and analytical about data, particularly when dealing with carbon emissions, which can feel abstract, like a new currency we're learning to navigate. *Who can visualise a tonne of CO2?* That may be why net zero seems distant or abstract. Yet, whether or not it feels immediately relevant, the reality is that net zero commitments increasingly impact business decisions, especially regarding Scope 3 emissions.

A sceptical voice might say, `This all sounds good in theory, but is carbon accounting really relevant to SMEs?' It's a fair question, but consider this: SMEs might lack dedicated sustainability experts., However, they have accountants who are perfectly positioned for this role. Accountants already provide analytical support for diverse business areas such as marketing spend, staff performance, product strategy, and customer feedback. Why wouldn't sustainability and net zero decision-making naturally fit into this advisory spectrum?

The evolving demands create challenges ideally suited to accountants' skill sets:

- Drilling down into data
- Validating or challenging data claims
- Seeking comprehensive supporting evidence before strategic decisions are reached

Our inherent professional scepticism means we don't simply accept claims at face value, especially when numbers are involved. That's where we excel, providing SMEs with critical, evidence-based insights.

Traditionally, our role has mainly focused on reporting historic data, offering insights into past events. However, forecasting and predictive insights are becoming increasingly important. Our predictive analysis ties directly into strategic planning, informing future pathways. This is particularly relevant for managing Scope 3 emissions, which aren't directly controlled but significantly influence a business's strategy and operations.

In November 2023, the ACCA published its professional insights report on the Chief Value Officer (CVO)[37]. It explains how accountants are uniquely positioned to provide broader business value beyond traditional financial oversight. This report suggested

---

[37] ACCA - Chief value officer - the important evolution of the CFO https://www.accaglobal.com/uk/en/professional-insights/global-profession/value-officer.html

accountants naturally function as trusted advisers across financial, social, environmental, and governance aspects.

This trusted-advisor role isn't new; sustainability is simply the next logical area where our advice adds value. They're a natural extension of these advisory responsibilities, integral to strategic decision-making rather than a separate specialism. We don't need to be sustainability experts any more than we need to be HR experts in guiding the setting and execution of business strategy.

While technology provides helpful carbon emissions calculators, these tools lack the nuanced insight accountants can offer. Our deep, contextual business understanding enables us to interpret why specific emissions patterns occur, such as specific increases due to business expansion. Technology alone can't provide this depth of knowledge, but accountants can. By translating data into strategic insights, we effectively bridge gaps that technology alone cannot address.

We can tell the story behind the numbers. Ethically.

Net Zero SWOT

Once you've grasped how to turn carbon data into meaningful insight, the next step is helping a business make sense of what to do about it. For both accountants in practice and those inside SMEs, this is where familiar strategic tools come into their own. One of the simplest and most powerful is the SWOT analysis.

We already use SWOT to explore commercial questions: where are we strong, where are we vulnerable, what could help us grow, and what might hold us back. The same tool can frame a conversation about net zero. It transforms sustainability from something abstract into a practical discussion that leads to action.

By viewing strengths, weaknesses, opportunities, and threats through a net zero lens, accountants can guide better decisions. This structure helps leadership teams move from good intentions to clear priorities, and it grounds the conversation in the kind of data-driven thinking we already excel at.

Before we start, it's worth remembering that healthy scepticism often surfaces in these conversations. That's not resistance; it's part of our job to explore it. Each question or challenge becomes a chance to deepen understanding and find a realistic way forward.

Strengths: recognising what's already working:

Many SMEs have strengths they don't yet see as part of their sustainability story. They've gone paperless, switched to cloud systems, or reduced travel because it made business sense. Those decisions are already cutting emissions. When accountants highlight these hidden wins, they show that progress is often closer than people think.

A client or colleague might ask, "Do these small changes really matter?" The answer is yes. They prove that emission reduction doesn't always mean disruption. Small, repeated actions build momentum and confidence for the bigger steps ahead.

Weaknesses: where improvements unlock value:

Every business has blind spots. Carbon data tends to shine a light on them. High energy costs, dependence on fossil fuels, or a lack of supplier information often point to inefficiencies that have financial implications as well as environmental ones.

Someone might say, "We can't afford the upfront cost of change." That's where we add real value. Accountants are experts in weighing short-term cost against long-term gain. We can show realistic payback periods, model the impact of grants or incentives, and turn what looks like a weakness into an investment case.

Opportunities: where progress meets profit:

Once weaknesses are clear, the conversation naturally turns to opportunities. These might include efficiency savings, product innovation, stronger supplier partnerships, or new market positioning. Many of these are within reach for SMEs, especially when guided by sound financial analysis.

A common question is, "Will customers really pay more for sustainability?" Evidence increasingly says they will. Consumers and corporate buyers alike are choosing low-carbon suppliers, and those preferences are shaping entire markets. By translating these trends into forecasts and performance metrics, accountants help businesses capture the opportunity instead of watching it pass by.

Threats: understanding and managing real risk:

Finally, every SWOT needs a reality check. Physical climate risks are growing, and so are regulatory and reputational pressures. Floods, energy shocks, and supply-chain disruptions are already affecting small businesses. Ignoring these risks doesn't make them go away; it simply leaves a business unprepared.

The question you'll often hear is, "Isn't this all too long-term to worry about?" The truth is that the long term has arrived. The businesses that plan ahead now will be the ones still standing when conditions change. Helping them anticipate risk is part of our professional duty.

Pulling it together:

A net zero SWOT isn't an academic exercise; it's a conversation starter that gives structure to complex issues. It helps an SME see where it stands today and where it can realistically go next. Whether you're an accountant advising clients or managing an in-house finance team, you already have the skills to facilitate it.

You're taking something familiar and applying it to a new challenge. That's the essence of this whole journey. Accountants don't need to become climate scientists to lead on net zero. We just need to use the tools we already trust to create clarity, confidence, and progress

CBA (Cost-benefit analysis)

When we talk about a Cost-Benefit Analysis, we're carefully weighing up each opportunity on its own merits. And that's something accountants are pretty good at, right?

Take energy supply, for instance. Many SMEs still rely heavily on fossil fuels; at first glance, this might feel like a significant weakness in a net zero plan. But let's flip that around. Could it be an opportunity in disguise? Imagine installing solar panels to reduce your dependence on traditional energy sources.

I know what you're thinking: *Hold on, the upfront costs are huge!* And yes, for many SMEs, this initial investment can seem daunting, especially when budgets are tight. However, the support from grants, government incentives, or even green financing options designed to encourage this type of investment can often be overlooked. Suddenly, the conversation shifts from `Can we afford this?' to `Why wouldn't we do this?'. It will only be the right choice for some, and who it is right for does also change over time.

The Hepworth Brewery case study later on will provide a brilliant example of this. They didn't just go for solar panels; they also implemented some genuinely innovative energy-saving measures. When energy prices skyrocketed after Russia's invasion of Ukraine, Hepworth Brewery didn't just survive; they thrived because they'd made these forward-thinking investments. By planning strategically, they'd built a cushion against volatility in the energy market, something competitors might've missed.

Now, onto the tricky bit: demonstrating clearly that long-term benefits outweigh the upfront costs. Here's where traditional valuation methods, like discounted cash flow (DCF), sometimes struggle. They tend to undervalue the long-term advantages of resilience and reputation that come with sustainable investments. But remember, as accountants, we can see beyond short-term horizons. We can look deeper, identifying strategic advantages like lower operating costs, greater resilience, and enhanced credibility throughout the entire supply chain.

Of course, some of your SME clients might push back, pointing out uncertainties around future energy prices or shifting government incentives. And fair enough, these are real concerns. However, scenario planning can help manage that uncertainty, and who is better equipped for scenario planning than an accountant? By stress-testing various potential outcomes, we can offer SMEs clarity and confidence, even amidst uncertainty.

And what about transport? If an SME has a sales team travelling hundreds of miles daily, switching to electric vehicles (EVs) probably isn't practical right now; it's not just about costs or range but also the reality of limited charging infrastructure. But if an SME mostly makes short, local trips? Suddenly, EVs don't just look greener; they're quite likely cheaper, too.

Sure, you could Google some generic answers about the costs and benefits of EVs or solar panels. But SMEs need more than that. They need you, someone who understands their unique situation and can weigh up costs, risks, and opportunities in the context of their specific business.

That's why SMEs rely on accountants. Because it's not just about numbers; it's about trusted insights that lead to better business decisions.

Case study: Hepworth Brewery – Raising a Glass to Net Zero

Based in West Sussex, Hepworth Brewery shows what an SME can achieve when it aligns its business strategy with a genuine commitment to sustainability. Brewing beer traditionally consumes vast amounts of energy, especially since heating and cooling are involved. However, founder Andy Hepworth wanted to challenge that convention from day one.

Sustainability was already at the heart of its design when Hepworth Brewery moved into its purpose-built home in 2016. Andy Hepworth's guiding principle was clear:

'I don't think you should damage the planet creating something for pleasure... If you can do it sustainably, then you absolutely should.

Economically, it makes sense too—maybe not overnight, but certainly over the long term.'

The brewery quickly put words into action, installing solar panels that significantly reduced its reliance on fossil fuels. Excess electricity is fed back into the grid, demonstrating how SMEs can contribute positively to their communities. But they didn't stop there. Hepworth Brewery installed advanced insulation, double glazing, and clever heat recovery systems, allowing them to double their production volumes while actually reducing their energy use.

One standout innovation is their high-temperature heat pump, the first of its kind in the UK brewing sector. This cutting-edge tech captures waste heat from boiling processes, recycles it to generate steam, and dramatically cuts fossil fuel use. Andy describes the potential of this project as `transformational, not only cutting emissions but significantly reducing our fuel costs too.'

Waste management is another strength. Spent grains and hops go directly to local farmers as animal feed, another win-win. Wastewater doesn't go down the drain either; it's treated through reed-bed filtration and a compact on-site anaerobic digester, converting brewery waste into renewable biogas. They even capture heat from beer chillers to warm their offices and visitor centre, implemented for around £300 of investment in equipment!

Hepworth Brewery's sustainable approach was further validated during the energy price spikes after Russia's invasion of Ukraine. Thanks to their investment in renewable energy and efficiency measures, the brewery was more resilient than competitors who were caught off-guard by sudden energy cost rises.

Today, Hepworth Brewery is regarded as one of the UK's leading sustainable SMEs. Their case study demonstrates the power of smart, strategic investment in sustainability. As Andy Hepworth proudly points out:

`Ultimately, sustainability isn't just good for the planet—it's good for business. It might take a little longer to see the benefits, but when you do, they really pay off.'

For SMEs considering their own net zero journeys, Hepworth Brewery provides a clear and inspiring example: start with a vision, think long-term, and the rewards, both environmental and financial, can be huge.

Professional ethics

Nobody is asking accountants to suddenly don green capes, grab a shield, and battle carbon emissions as reborn eco-warriors. That's not our role, nor should it be. But perhaps it's time for a little reflection. Our professional ethics clearly guide us to act with integrity, objectivity, and always in the best interests of our clients and their businesses. Yet, what does that really mean in the context of sustainability and the net zero transition?

As accountants, our primary duty has always been to offer objective, impartial advice based on sound financial analysis. Our role doesn't explicitly require us to champion the green agenda, but here's where things get interesting. Influential figures like BlackRock's Larry Fink have clearly stated that sustainability isn't about being environmentally virtuous; it's about financial prudence. His famous assertion that `climate risk is investment risk' is not mere rhetoric. It highlights that failing to account for sustainability and climate risks can seriously jeopardise long-term profitability and viability.

While our professional code of ethics doesn't specifically mandate that we prioritise sustainability, perhaps there's room for reflection here. If we, as accountants, aren't considering sustainability factors like climate risk in our everyday advice, are we genuinely fulfilling our professional duty to our clients? We don't need to transform ourselves into sustainability experts overnight, but our inherent skills - objectivity, professional scepticism, analytical rigour - uniquely equip us to raise these critical questions.

This distinction matters because many SMEs have unintentionally drifted into greenwashing, not through malicious intent but through misunderstanding terminology or misjudging the impacts of their actions. An SME might innocently claim its packaging is sustainable because it is made from recyclable materials. However, as we've seen from cases involving more prominent companies, such claims can quickly unravel and cause reputational harm.

And that's precisely where accountants can step in, using our ethical framework as a practical guide. With a comprehensive view across an SME's data and operations, we can help businesses stay accurate, truthful, and credible when discussing their net zero ambitions. We can act as a thoughtful sounding board, preventing overreaching claims and ensuring decisions align clearly with the facts.

Ultimately, it's not about making accountants into superheroes; it's simply about doing what we already excel at, but through the lens of sustainability. That might not explicitly be defined in our ethics code yet, but perhaps it should be part of how we think about our professional competence today.

No superhero capes required, just accountants doing what we do best, carefully and ethically guiding SMEs through the challenges ahead.

Summary

Our clients often turn to us because they trust us to make sense of complexity. Whether interpreting financial figures or helping to clarify operational puzzles, SMEs already depend heavily on our unique expertise. So, stepping into the net zero advisory role isn't a radical leap; it's a natural progression.

At the turn of the 21st century, the idea of accountants leading on sustainability or net zero strategies seemed pretty far-fetched. Yet here we are, uniquely placed to guide SMEs through the complexities of emissions data and strategic planning. As accountants, we can:

- Drill down into emissions data, even when it seems intangible or unclear.
- Challenge assumptions and claims, ensuring accuracy and credibility.
- Provide valuable insights to inform strategic business decisions, helping SMEs feel confident and clear about the choices ahead.

In fact, I'd bet many SMEs are already on the net zero path without realising it. They've already made smart business decisions, like moving to cloud-based solutions or going paperless, without even thinking about emissions. Your job, then, is to help them see that these steps are part of a bigger, brighter picture, one where net zero is attainable and beneficial. And then show them what their next step is. And the one after that.

It's all about perspective. By helping your SME clients see the familiar through a slightly different lens, using skills you already possess, you become the catalyst that helps them unlock new opportunities and safeguard against future risks.

You don't need a superhero cape to do this, you just need to be you: an accountant who is trusted, capable, insightful, and, yes, genuinely awesome.

Ready for the next challenge? In Chapter 6, we'll explore how to measure all of this effectively. After all, what gets measured gets managed, right? And that's where accountants truly shine.

CHAPTER 6

MEASUREMENT

Estimation vs Precision

If the first milestone in achieving a Science-Based Target is a 50% reduction by 2030, it begs the question; 50% of what? We need a measurement. We need a **baseline**. But what does measuring CO2e emissions even look like?

Well, let's not kid ourselves. By `measuring', what we really mean is `estimating.' And honestly, that's perfectly okay. We shouldn't get hung up on the idea that an estimate needs to be 100% accurate. If we did, we'd never get started at all. Estimates are pretty much all we've got to work with to progress, and they're more than sufficient to give us valuable figures and insights. These insights will guide us in prioritising actions effectively.

I'd even argue that while highly accurate carbon measurements are possible, they often involve costly, complex, and frankly unnecessary methods for SMEs. Remember, maximum accuracy isn't the goal here.

Reduction is the goal.

And this is still accounting, just not the reconcile-to-a-penny version. The principles remain the same, even though, as I've already noted, the language of carbon accounting differs from our usual expectations. We're already well on our way as long as we're comfortable working with estimates rather than precise measurements. And let's face it, accountants already know how to deal with estimates. It's practically our bread and butter.

A sceptical voice might say, *If it's just an estimate, isn't it meaningless?* Well, no. An informed estimate is infinitely better than a blank sheet of paper. It signals to stakeholders that your business has begun its net zero journey. Your intent is clear, and that alone can carry weight in contract negotiations, funding decisions, and your reputation with clients and investors.

In fact, estimating is just the start; once we've got these numbers, we can drill down, ask smarter questions, and prioritise effectively. How exactly do we do that? Let's look at some practical tools and approaches next.

In short, accountants are perfectly placed for this task. Interpreting numbers to make strategic decisions is literally our day job, so applying this to net zero isn't fundamentally different from what we already excel at.

Remember, this isn't about perfection; it's about actionable insights, and that's exactly what we'll unlock next.

Practical Tools and Approaches

Every expense line in a typical P&L statement can be translated into estimated carbon emissions using an emission factor. This means applying an established multiplier to your spending, turning pounds into kilograms of CO2e.

Spend-based methods:

Spend-based methodologies are quick, straightforward, and especially helpful when you're just getting started since they use readily accessible data. They translate the financial data from your accounting system into emissions. Here are two excellent resources:

- **The Greenhouse Gas Protocol:** A globally recognised framework with established spend-based coefficients. Simply enter your expenses, and it returns estimated emissions. It's a great place to start, though the factors are aggregated and not supplier-specific.
- **SWC Multi-Regional Input-Output (MRIO) Model:** Developed by sustainability expert Mike Berners-Lee (yes, inventor-of-the-internet Tim's brother), this tool uses publicly available data to offer emissions factors across 103 industries and 65 countries. It is ideal for more detailed spend-based insights, especially if your business operates internationally.

These spend-based datasets can vary across territories, so it's worth checking what's most applicable to your region or industry. But remember, this manual approach can feel burdensome, especially if the SME's priority for the week is clawing together the cash to fund payroll.

That's where more automated tools come in. Platforms like **Sage Carbon Accounting** plug directly into your accounting software, automatically doing much of the heavy lifting. You enter basic activity information, and they deliver instant, easy-to-understand emissions snapshots. It's perfect if you're looking to reduce hassle and get immediate insights to act upon.

If you encounter unusually high emissions in certain areas of a business, bringing in a specialist consultant might make sense. They can provide deeper analysis for specific activities, giving you more detailed insights and actions.

There are hundreds of such tools, ranging from completely free to low-cost subscriptions and consultant-led options. For an up-to-date listing, visit https://jameslizars.com/blog or the plug-ins directory for your ledger software, which regularly reviews and updates tools specifically suited to SMEs.

Remember, your first step isn't about getting measurement-perfect. It's about using these tools to make informed estimates, highlight areas for improvement, and refine your approach as you go. That way, you're actively progressing towards your net zero goal, step by manageable step.

How does carbon accounting work?

Sage Carbon Accounting

Duncan Oswald, Sage Climate Science Lead

The first thing to say about carbon accounting is that it's not an exact science, and there is no such thing as a completely accurate carbon footprint. At Sage, we prefer to think of it as creating the best estimate possible with the available data and methods.

It's also important to say that this doesn't devalue the exercise as, although measurement might be required for reporting, or similar, purposes it's really a means to an end with the ultimate goal being to reduce emissions and mitigate climate change. Carbon accounting, whilst not exact, can still provide a huge amount of insight into where we need to focus our energy.

So, how does carbon accounting work? In a nutshell, it is based on the process of taking the amount of a certain spend or activity and multiplying it by what's called an emissions factor. This is a coefficient that represents the average GHG emissions per unit of spend or activity. For example, spending a pound with an accountant in the UK results (on average) in the emission of around 86g of CO2 e. Add that up across all of a business's spend and activity and you have an estimate of the business's carbon footprint.

As mentioned, carbon accounting can take an amount of spend or activity. These are two of the most common ways to calculate emissions. A spend based methodology can be used by automatically pulling through data from an accounting solution, using AI, and other technology, to match transactions to the right emissions factor and then calculating the associated emissions. That's great for purchased goods and services, which often make up the majority of a business's footprint, and some other emission categories but it needs to be supplemented by an activity based methodology. This is very similar to spend based but instead of being a pound unit, it would be another unit dependent on the activity. This could either be used to give a better estimate than possible with spend or to fill in gaps where a spend based methodology isn't possible as the activity doesn't show up in a business's accounts. An example of this is employee commuting. The unit might be the number of employees, or for a better estimate, the miles travelled by employees across different modes of transport.

From the above, it may be clear that the key to carbon accounting is the availability of data. Accurate, detailed accounts and records of other business activities are vital inputs. Applying the most relevant and granular emissions factor, and doing so in as automated a fashion as possible, creates the best estimate of a business's footprint.

Although continually improving, emissions factors are currently only available at a fairly aggregated level so, for example, spend on materials can have an emissions factor based on the type of material but not the exact product from a specific supplier. This means this approach will only get you so far. If you spend money with two different suppliers for the same goods, they will both given the same factor. This will give you an idea of the emissions associated with those goods, relative to other activities, but it doesn't help you choose the supplier with the lowest emissions. To do that, you need a specific factor for each: then you can favour the one with the lowest emissions, and so reduce your own emissions. This is the future in carbon accounting: an automated network of robust, live emissions factors that will dramatically increase our ability to make more accurate estimates of business emissions, and to reduce them. The more businesses that start estimating their emissions, the closer we get to this future.

Practical Application and Examples (Thrive snapshot)

As accountants, we're often pigeon-holed as specialists in monetary transactions, the usual debits, credits, and reconciliations. But we regularly handle non-financial data too. Sure, this data isn't always 100% accurate, but we know how to work effectively with estimates, because that's the available data. Just think of those classic exam scenarios: activity-based costing in a manufacturing setup or analysing timesheets to measure profitability in professional services. Handling uncertainty isn't new to us; we acknowledge inaccuracies, minimise them, and tailor our conclusions accordingly.

Applying these familiar principles to carbon accounting is straightforward. When you feed your P&L and other operational data into a carbon accounting tool, you get a clear snapshot of your emissions sources categorised by Scope. You'll see how different activities - employee commuting and homeworking, office energy, software, supplies, and equipment purchases - contribute to your footprint. Often, these tools let you drill down further into particular suppliers or individual transactions for better insights.

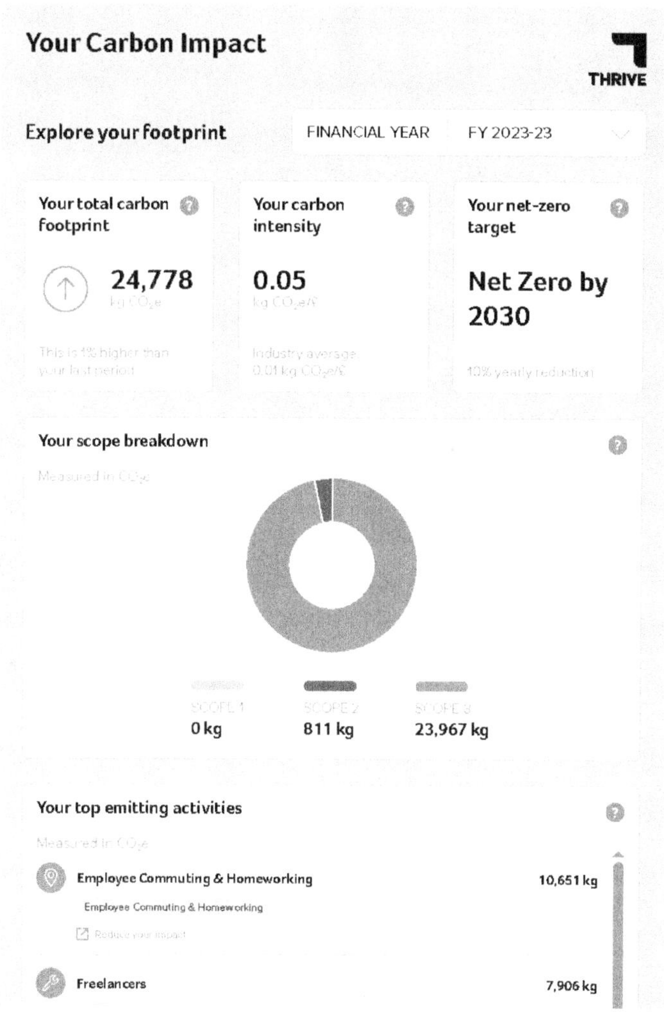

Fig. 2 Thrive carbon accounting dashboard

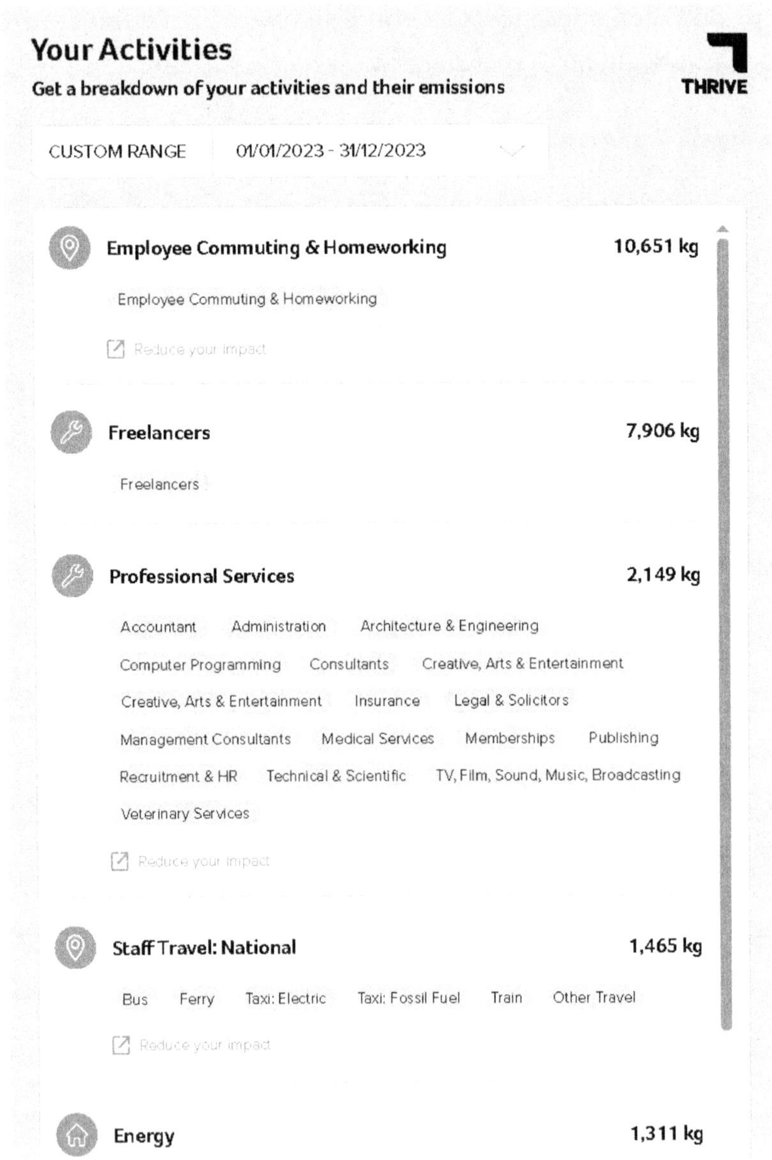

Fig.3 Thrive carbon accounting drilldown

Here's what it looked like for my own business, Thrive. When we plugged our data into Sage Earth (now Sage Carbon Accounting), our top emission source immediately stood out: employee commuting and homeworking. Initially, this surprised us. With a small team of eight people (including an overseas team member who alone represents 50% of this category!), it quickly became clear that addressing commuting and homeworking emissions could significantly move the needle. This insight shaped our strategic priorities, prompting us to encourage renewable energy tariffs at home and reduce unnecessary travel.

Remember, the goal here isn't to achieve perfect precision; it's about getting a clear enough picture to know where to prioritise your efforts. And this is where accountants naturally excel: interpreting the numbers and turning insights into actionable strategies.

Take travel as another example. Spend-based methods have their flaws here. For instance, booking train tickets just a couple of weeks ahead often appears to lower your emissions according to a spend-based model simply because tickets are cheaper compared to last-minute bookings. Clearly, the emissions from a train journey don't change based on when the ticket is bought, that's illogical and won't sit well with most accountants.

So, what's better? Activity-based measurement. This approach tracks actual emissions based on distance travelled, mode of transport, and specific journey details. Modern travel booking systems often incorporate real-time emissions data at the point of purchase, giving businesses accurate, journey-specific carbon footprints. This approach allows for genuinely informed decisions, rather than decisions skewed by pricing anomalies.

The main point of all these numbers and insights isn't to automatically start with the most significant emission source; it's about identifying the easiest, quickest, or most impactful changes you can make first. That's how SMEs and their accountants can practically approach carbon measurement.

Activity-based Measurement

While spend-based methods give us a useful start, they can quickly reveal some oddities, like the train ticket example we discussed earlier. To tackle those flaws, we can move towards activity-based measurement, where we directly measure the business's real-world actions and outputs rather than relying solely on financial data.

For instance, in Scope 2 emissions (those from purchased energy), using actual kWh from your energy bills rather than spend-based estimates significantly improves accuracy. It is straightforward, as you're reading off your bill and applying the appropriate emissions factor.

Scope 1 emissions (direct emissions from owned assets, like company vehicles or machinery) similarly benefit from direct measurement. Here, tracking actual fuel consumption or metering specific equipment usage provides a far clearer picture than a general spend-based figure.

Regarding business travel, shifting from spend-based estimates to tools tracking actual mileage, vehicle type, or flight details will yield significantly more accurate results. Modern booking tools often embed carbon calculators, immediately clarifying emissions for each journey. Maybe travel is only a small proportion of your emissions, and a spend-based approach is good enough, provided it's paired with actions that reduce emissions.

The real challenge kicks in for purchased goods and services (also Scope 3). Engaging directly with suppliers to obtain detailed emissions data about the products or services provided will greatly enhance the accuracy of your measurements, but let's be realistic, it's also where SMEs find the process most challenging. Suppliers may not have this data available, and it can be burdensome to gather. Who would you phone at Microsoft to find out the emissions factor for MS Office? How would your marketing agency respond?

It sounds like it might be a futile exercise, but what's valuable about it is that asking the question may not immediately get you the data you need, but it's how a chain reaction starts. What happens when someone else also asks the question, and someone else beyond that? How long before that supplier speaks to their accountant and asks for help answering questions? And then they ask their suppliers for better data?

Ask the question anyway.

Realistically, this is where it's helpful to talk about Life Cycle Analysis (LCA), a process that assesses a product's full emissions from creation to disposal. But let's keep our expectations realistic. LCA can be incredibly data-intensive, and for SMEs, it's about striking the right balance between greater accuracy and the resources needed to achieve it. The effort might feel substantial, yet the insights gained, particularly for products and services that significantly impact your emissions, can be game-changing.

Ultimately, moving towards more activity-based measurement in your highest-impact areas doesn't just sharpen accuracy; it equips you to make smarter decisions, which in turn get us closer to meaningful emissions reductions.

Product Life Cycle Analysis (LCA)

We've discussed activity-based measurements and sharpening our estimates, but what about SMEs that produce or sell physical products? How can an accountant help these businesses understand and communicate the emissions embedded in their products? That's precisely where **Product Lifecycle Analysis (LCA)** comes into play.

Think of LCA as telling a product's entire story, from sourcing raw materials and manufacturing processes through transport, product use, and finally disposal or recycling. It's detailed and thorough, pinpointing exactly where emissions are hiding throughout a product's lifecycle.

But let's acknowledge something upfront: conducting a full-scale LCA can feel overwhelming for most SMEs. It demands time, resources, and detailed data collection, perfect for multinational corporations with dedicated sustainability teams, but daunting for smaller businesses juggling limited resources.

So why raise the topic at all?

Two compelling reasons:

Firstly, if you're advising or working within an SME that procures products, even basic lifecycle thinking can help pinpoint major emission hotspots. Full-blown LCAs aren't always necessary. Often, identifying products with inherently high emissions due to complex supply chains, intensive processing, or overseas transport is enough to drive significant improvement.

Secondly (and perhaps more importantly), SMEs producing or selling products increasingly face requests from their customers, especially larger organisations already pursuing net zero targets, for detailed product emissions data. The faster these SMEs anticipate and respond to these data demands, the better positioned they'll be.

Picture the conversation when an SME is already prepared:

Customer: `Do you have carbon emissions data for these products?'

SME: `Absolutely. We've already completed simplified lifecycle analyses on our core products and can provide exactly the information you need.'

Suddenly, they're no longer just another supplier; they've become trusted partners who proactively meet customers' data needs. That's a significant competitive advantage, making them stand out clearly from their peers.

However, as accountants, either within the SME or advising externally, how can we realistically support businesses engaging with LCA without incurring excessive costs?

- **Start small, stay strategic:** Recommend SMEs identify their flagship or highest-demand products first. There's no need for exhaustive analysis; target those products that significantly impact their carbon emissions or matter most to customers.
- **Leverage existing resources:** Many sectors already provide industry-specific LCA databases and emission benchmarks.

Encourage businesses to tap into these resources first, rather than starting from scratch.

- **Engage proactively with suppliers:** Advise SMEs to ask suppliers for any available emissions data. Businesses don't need deep sustainability expertise to start these conversations - they simply need to ask clearly for available information.

Yes, robust product-level emissions data can be sparse, especially for SMEs. But remember, each request made and each dataset shared triggers that chain reaction we've discussed earlier. Suppliers and businesses up and down the value chain soon realise that providing emissions transparency isn't optional, it's essential.

And who's perfectly placed to guide SMEs through this journey? That's right, accountants. Our profession specialises in interpreting data, asking insightful questions, and assisting businesses in communicating clearly and effectively.

The goal here isn't perfection or conducting detailed LCAs for every product. Instead, it's about encouraging lifecycle thinking strategically, helping SMEs identify emission hotspots, respond confidently to customer expectations, and maintain their competitive edge.

Transparency is fast becoming non-negotiable. SMEs guided by informed accountants today will be the ones positioned strongly tomorrow.

Handling Growth and Intensity vs Absolute Measures

When Thrive first used a carbon accounting tool (Sage Earth in our case), it integrated smoothly with our Xero data. I initially ran our numbers over a lunch break, refining them later with more detail. We'd already taken some significant actions, so I tracked the impact back over three years:

- **IT and office furniture:** We almost wiped out emissions here by choosing high-quality refurbished equipment, and we began monitoring the actual electricity usage of our devices.
- **Employee commuting and freelancers:** We offered incentives for renewable energy tariffs at home and provided smart plugs to eliminate standby energy waste.
- **Staff travel:** We actively minimised travel and opted for train journeys instead of flights or personal vehicles whenever practical.

All good so far, except that, despite the actions, the numbers went up year on year.

Yes, you read that correctly. Even with those actions, our emissions **increased**.

Why? Simply put, growth. Our firm is consistently growing, adding team members, and every scenario I looked at indicated that absolute emissions would inevitably rise in the near term. I'm being transparent here because accountants must grapple openly with this reality.

You may have heard the concept of `degrowth', positioned in the context that endlessly pursuing growth in a world of finite-resources isn't sustainable. Intellectually, it's compelling. But even in this green transition, degrowth sounds radical, especially for SMEs. We're currently dealing with today's reality and constraints, including ambitious net zero targets.

Some environmentally minded readers might cringe here, and I get it. Deep and rapid absolute emissions reduction is required. But SMEs, by their very nature, are volatile; they're often either fighting to survive or ambitiously expanding, and insisting strictly on absolute reductions clashes fundamentally with their core objectives.

So here's where I believe accountants can genuinely add value. Instead of focusing only on absolute emissions, we can encourage SMEs to measure and manage their emissions intensity, essentially emissions relative to revenue or headcount. Yes, intensity metrics might initially feel like a convenient way to dodge responsibility. But let's look closer:

In practical terms, intensity metrics encourage smarter, leaner growth. If greener SMEs grow faster by taking market share from less sustainable competitors, sector-wide emissions drop, even if some individual businesses temporarily emit more in absolute terms. This isn't avoiding responsibility; it's strategic emissions management that aligns directly with SME goals.

I'll admit, this took me years to reconcile. But accountants understand business reality: we can't magically stop SMEs from growing, nor should we. Instead, our expertise lies in enabling smarter decisions that balance growth with emissions accountability. We can advocate for systems change, we can promote a macro-economic rethink along the lines of Kate Raworth's excellent book, Doughnut Economics[38], but day to day we're working within the status quo.

How exactly do we do this?

Just as you project financial growth, like revenue per head or team costs versus turnover, we can project emissions growth through intensity metrics. Let's say an SME plans to install an air-source heat pump. As accountants, we can reflect that planned capital investment directly into emissions intensity forecasts. We track how emissions intensity would evolve from the baseline, clearly showing what reductions result from specific actions.

This is a powerful narrative. It's transparent, credible, and aligned with the realities of SME growth. You don't have to disclose sensitive financial details either; intensity metrics can be shared independently, maintaining confidentiality while demonstrating genuine commitment.

What's the alternative? SMEs repeatedly postponing their net zero targets, relying heavily on offsets, or pretending that growth and emissions reduction can never coexist. None of these options inspires trust.

Instead, by thoughtfully using intensity measures, SMEs build credible, transparent strategies that genuinely move them closer to net zero. Because of our skills in analysis, forecasting, and clear communication, accountants are perfectly placed to drive this strategic approach, ethically.

It's a nuanced path, but the realistic, pragmatic way forward.

---

38 https://www.kateraworth.com/ Doughnut Economics

And accountants are precisely the right professionals to lead SMEs along it.

Target Setting and Measurement Challenges

If we're serious about making progress towards science-based targets, we clearly need figures to measure against. But let's face it, getting started can feel daunting, I've been there myself.

When I began my own net zero journey in 2022, I wasn't exactly thrilled at the idea of measuring our emissions. As a panellist at Accountex London that year, I recall speaking against measurement as a priority. The reason? At that time, accessible carbon accounting tools designed specifically for SMEs simply weren't available. Instead, my only option seemed to be a massive spreadsheet created by the Carbon Trust. Now, if you're anything like me, the thought of wrestling with someone else's sprawling spreadsheet fills you with dread. You spend half your time figuring out what the creator was thinking.

This particular spreadsheet aimed to be a one-size-fits-all solution for every sector, every type of business, across the entire UK. This was hugely overwhelming and mostly irrelevant for a small accounting business like mine. Instead of clarity, it offered complexity and noise, frustrating and practically pointless.

But here's the important bit: instead of getting stuck on measurement perfection, I realised it was better to take immediate, practical actions, actions I knew would reduce emissions regardless of the initial measurement quality. My thinking was simple: start taking steps now and trust that better tools would soon become available. When they did, I could always retrospectively apply these newer, more accurate methods to my historical data to track our real progress.

And sure enough, that's what happened. More intuitive, SME-friendly carbon accounting tools arrived, making the whole process more manageable and insightful. Thankfully, I'd already gathered the data, so updating previous measurements with better methodology was straightforward.

Waiting for perfection is never the answer. Action beats waiting every time. Estimates, especially informed, thoughtful ones, are powerful. They give us direction, inform decisions, and most importantly, they let us get started.

At the time of writing, there's still plenty of room for improvement in carbon accounting tools, particularly around enabling detailed, accurate net zero projections. Even the phrase `carbon accounting' feels misleading since it's not purely financial data we're dealing with. However, the real value lies in the non-financial insights we can gain, which help us make smarter decisions about the future.

So, our job as accountants isn't to wait until the perfect tool arrives; it's to ensure we've gathered good, consistent data right now, so that as tools improve, our projections become ever more meaningful and precise. Think of it as any other business forecast you might prepare: what happens if a business invests in renewable energy? What if they switch to low-energy lighting or introduce electric vehicles?

Every strategic decision we make now should prompt us to ask how much closer the business will get to achieving its 50% emissions reduction target by 2030. That's the real value of measurement, not perfection, but actionable insight guiding better business choices.

Summary

When performing a carbon emissions estimation for SMEs, the traditional idea of measurement isn't particularly helpful in its most precise and exact form. What matters is achieving consistency and comparability from one period to the next. At first glance, the CO_2e numbers might seem vague. After all, it's challenging to visualise what a tonne of CO_2 actually looks like. Is it the size of a football pitch? A double-decker bus?

Instead, the true value of these numbers lies in the questions they prompt you and your clients to ask:

- Are emissions improving or getting worse over time?
- How do they stack up against industry peers?
- Which changes could influence future emissions significantly?

The answers to these questions will highlight the primary sources of emissions and point clearly to areas where meaningful action can be taken.

At Thrive, for example, we discovered that around 5% of our footprint came from travel. Even though we didn't travel extensively, identifying this allowed us to find practical ways to reduce it. And here's the brilliant thing about spend-based carbon footprint estimation: lower emissions usually mean lower costs. Wherever SMEs can identify opportunities to cut emissions, a strong business case often writes itself.

Remember, the aim isn't just producing a number; it's about what that number prompts SMEs to consider next. Rather than starting with the most significant emission source, focusing initially on the areas that promise the quickest or most practical reductions makes sense.

The closer SMEs get to achieving their net zero goals, the less significant minor inaccuracies in initial estimations become. Dealing with uncertainty and complexity is second nature to accountants; it's exactly what we're good at. Our analytical skills align with this process, positioning us as ideal advisors to guide SMEs through their net zero journey.

Throughout the book, we've explored the educational foundation, clearly articulated the business case, and demonstrated why accountants are so ideally placed to support SMEs on the net zero path. Now it's time to move from insight to action. In the next chapter, we'll delve into how accountants can practically guide SMEs to set credible targets, embed meaningful reductions, and implement their net zero plans.

CHAPTER 7

THE PLAN

What does a credible plan for net zero look like?

We've already learned that creating a credible net zero plan isn't only about internal business requirements. It's equally important to consider third-party stakeholders (lenders, customers, and investors) who need this information to support their own transition planning.

The Transition Plan Taskforce (TPT)[39] launched by HM Treasury in March 2022, brought together industry, academia, and regulators to develop good practice for transition plan disclosures across finance and the real economy. Primarily aimed at larger organisations, the TPT provides a gold-standard framework for transition planning. Yet, SMEs can still adopt (and adapt) key principles from this framework for their own purposes.

---

[39] https://transitiontaskforce.net/disclosure-framework/

Supported by the ISSB (International Sustainability Standards Board), the TPT aligns closely with IFRS (International Financial Reporting Standards), standards already fundamental to our roles as accountants. It's important to note that the TPT is not a climate activist manifesto; rather, it's a structured framework firmly grounded in familiar accounting terminology.

Although SMEs may not fully replicate every aspect of the TPT framework, we can adapt it to suit our specific contexts. Key aspects that SMEs can readily address include:

1. Climate considerations
2. Greenhouse gas emissions
3. Carbon credits

In this chapter, I outline how SMEs can develop practical, achievable plans incorporating these elements into three distinct, actionable areas:

- Ambition
- Action
- Accountability

Ambition

First things first, let's talk about ambition. What's your target?

A great starting point is aiming for a 50% reduction by 2030. It's widely recognised and lines up neatly with the Science Based Targets initiative (SBTi). And why SBTi? Well, mainly because that's what your clients, suppliers, and stakeholders will increasingly expect from you. They're going to ask, so let's get ready for it.

Now, as you kick off your planning, you'll quickly spot opportunities to reach that 50% sooner than you might think. But let's be honest, the second 50% will likely be tougher, involving a few trade-offs along the way, not least carbon offsets. The good news is that after 2030, broader trends like a cleaner energy grid and new technologies should help bridge the gap towards that full net zero target by 2050. But for now, just keep your eyes on that first milestone: cutting emissions in half before 2030.

How do you set your specific target? Easy, you start by measuring where you're at right now. Use one of the user-friendly carbon accounting tools we talked about earlier. And don't worry, these tools are so intuitive, you can probably get your baseline sorted within an hour; they plug straight into your accounting software and they increasingly use AI tooling to churn through the groundwork. At the very least, these tools will give you an overview of your emissions across Scopes 1, 2, and 3. But the good stuff happens when you dive deeper. You'll see how your suppliers stack up, and get detailed breakdowns of how different activities, like employee commuting, remote working, equipment purchases, or software usage, impact your emissions. Trust me, seeing that breakdown will show you clearly where the quick wins are hiding.

Action

Now that you've set your targets, the real fun starts, turning ambition into action. But how exactly do you do that? Let's break it down clearly into three categories: **Now, Next, and Later**.

Now – Quick Wins (Scope 1 and 2)

Here's the excellent news: you have direct control over your Scope 1 and 2 emissions, so there are straightforward actions you can tackle immediately:

- **Switch to a renewable energy tariff** (if you manage your energy contracts).
- **Upgrade to energy-efficient LED lighting.**
- **Implement smart heating controls** like thermostats or timers.
- **Encourage your team to switch to renewable energy at home**, which is especially beneficial if you have remote workers.
- **Choose pre-owned or refurbished office furniture and IT equipment.**
- **Go completely paperless**, or as close as you can manage. Digital ledgers beat shoe boxes of receipts anyway.
- **Switch your website to green hosting.** Yes, really. The internet uses over 416 terawatt-hours globally each year, that's more electricity than the entire UK consumes annually! Curious about your website's footprint? Check it now at websitecarbon.com.

Next – A Little More Effort but Bigger Rewards

These steps might take a bit more legwork, but they're powerful:

- **Work with your landlord** to switch to renewable electricity if they control your premises' energy supply.

- **Analyse your supply chain** by spend to see which suppliers already have credible net zero plans. Knowing this helps you effectively prioritise your next steps.

Later – The Long Game (Scope 3)

Let's discuss Scope 3. SMEs technically only need to commit to reducing these indirect emissions because they're not under direct control. But here's the catch, many of your customers, especially larger ones, will demand more.

Take my own business, Thrive. Our main suppliers, Sage and Xero, are already committed to solid net zero targets (great news!). But then there's Dext, our second-largest software spend. As of writing, their sustainability commitment is vague at best, which leaves me with a tricky decision: do I stick with Dext, hoping they'll eventually step up, or do I switch as soon as a more proactive competitor emerges?

That's the real challenge SMEs face. But rather than seeing this as a frustration, view it as leverage. The more we collectively push, the faster suppliers will align their strategies with ours.

Later – Nudging the Big Guys

Influencing larger suppliers without clear sustainability plans isn't easy, but it's not impossible either. Regularly ask your suppliers about their net zero intentions. You might not get immediate results, but consistent pressure works wonders over time.

Let's be realistic: SMEs don't always have the luxury to switch suppliers instantly, especially if alternatives aren't up to scratch. But keep monitoring the market. If greener alternatives become available, jump on them.

I faced exactly this dilemma with Dext and decided to wait it out (for now). However, switching becomes much more attractive if a competitor emerges with a credible sustainability plan or if Sage and Xero enhance their pre-accounting offerings.

Don't underestimate the power of your influence. Every question, every nudge, creates momentum.

Initially, I worried these small changes were trivial, almost too easy. But small actions stack up quickly. And as a bonus, I've become far more fluent in carbon accounting, making it easier to guide clients through their journeys. We'll look at these client conversations in Chapter 10

Accountability

One of the most significant risks in any transition plan isn't the targets you set or even the initial actions you take; it's whether you actually follow through. And let's be honest: without accountability, even the best-laid plans can quickly fade into the background, forgotten in the whirlwind of day-to-day business.

So, what does accountability really mean in the context of an SME's net zero plan? It means being open, transparent, and honest about your progress. You don't need glossy reports or complicated dashboards, just clear, simple updates that you share regularly with your team, clients, and suppliers. Think of it as telling the ongoing story of your journey, complete with successes, setbacks, and everything in between.

Here's a straightforward template you can easily adopt:

Example Co: Net Zero Progress Report

Goal: Achieve a 50% emissions reduction by 2030 and net zero emissions by 2050

Baseline KPI: Tons of CO_2e per employee

Actions Taken:

- Installed energy-efficient LED lighting throughout the office
- Adopted policy only to buy refurbished computer equipment

Annual Progress Update:

Year	Employees	Total Emissions	Emissions per Employee	Progress vs. Baseline
2023	10	10,000 kg	1,000 kg	Baseline
2024	15	13,500 kg	900 kg	10% decrease

What We Learned: Yes, our absolute emissions went up slightly due to business growth, but our intensity metric showed a clear improvement, exactly what we aimed for. We made tangible progress without disrupting our operations by simply swapping out lighting and switching to refurbished computer equipment.

Looking Ahead: Next year, we'll work closely with our suppliers to ensure they are aligned with our net zero goals. We've identified supplier engagement as our biggest opportunity to accelerate progress.

Regularly publishing simple updates like this, both internally and externally, has powerful benefits:

- **Builds Trust:** Stakeholders love transparency; being open earns you credibility.
- **Keeps Momentum:** Regular updates keep everyone motivated and focused on your goals.
- **Unlocks Improvement:** Regular reflection naturally surfaces new ideas and opportunities to push your plan forward.

As accountants, you're perfectly positioned to tell the story behind the numbers, making the net zero journey both practical and compelling for your stakeholders. Accountability is key to execution.

So, embrace it. Share the journey, celebrate the progress, and stay open about the challenges. An SME's net zero story is worth telling, and who better to tell it than you?

Summary

Let's be clear, having a plan is just the beginning. Accountability is what brings a net zero plan to life. It transforms intentions into measurable progress and ensures commitments aren't forgotten in the daily rush of running an SME. By regularly measuring and openly sharing progress, wins, and challenges, you build trust with stakeholders, keep the momentum going, and make your plan tangible and credible. Remember, accountability isn't about perfection; it's about transparency, continuous improvement, and authentically telling your net zero story. Because ultimately, this journey matters, and your role as an accountant in guiding SMEs through it has never been more important.

Now, let's dive into Chapter 8 and explore how you turn this concept of accountability into real momentum.

CHAPTER 8

EXECUTION

Now that you've set your ambition, identified clear actions, and defined your accountability framework, it's time to bring your net zero plan to life. If a goal without a plan is just a wish, then a plan without execution is just another forgotten document collecting dust.

In Chapter 7, we explored what a credible SME net zero plan looks like, setting measurable targets, prioritising impactful actions, and communicating transparently with your stakeholders. You've laid the groundwork. You've built your roadmap. But let's face it: planning is often the easy part. The real test comes in the execution, turning your ideas into daily actions that genuinely move the needle towards your targets.

This chapter is about just that, practical execution. We'll dive into how you can seamlessly embed net zero practices into your daily operations, manage your progress through structured 90-day reviews, and adapt as circumstances evolve. You'll see how being agile and responsive isn't a sign of a flawed plan, but rather the hallmark of an SME serious about its net zero commitments.

Let's get practical.

Practical Execution Tips: Making Net Zero a Daily Habit

Let's get real for a minute. The truth about achieving net zero isn't in grand gestures or sweeping declarations; it's hidden in your everyday routine. It's about making simple changes that quietly become part of your daily business activities.

Here are some easy ways you can weave net zero into your day-to-day:

- **Make net zero a standing item on meeting agendas**
  This doesn't mean turning every meeting into a climate summit. Just spend five minutes checking progress against your net zero actions, whether it's quick wins, new challenges, or sharing an update. It's incredible how accountability builds when you discuss it openly and regularly.

- **Integrate net zero thinking into your processes**
  When you're about to make a purchase, ask yourself: *Is there a lower-carbon option?* Whether it's office supplies, tech, or even catering, this simple habit nudges every decision towards sustainability.

- **Give clear, manageable tasks to your team**
  Delegate net zero actions directly to the people best placed to

handle them. If Jane looks after procurement, let Jane research eco-friendly suppliers. If Ahmed manages facilities, get him to handle switching to energy-efficient lighting. Trust your team to handle this, they'll appreciate the clarity and autonomy.

- **Leverage quarterly reviews (you're already doing them!)**
  We love a 90-day plan, right? So, just slot your net zero goals into those reviews. It doesn't need a special meeting, just a quick quarterly health check to see what's working, what's not, and what you might try next.

- **Celebrate the small wins publicly**
  Don't underestimate the power of sharing your wins. Switched your lighting? Reduced your travel emissions? Go ahead and shout about it on LinkedIn or your website. Small actions inspire more small actions.

Remember, none of these steps are rocket science; they're common sense, practical, and totally doable, even in a busy SME environment. The real power comes from making net zero feel normal, not exceptional.

As accountants, we're uniquely skilled at this, taking something that seems complicated and embedding it naturally into the flow of everyday business.

Procurement and Supplier Engagement: Using Influence Wisely

Let's talk about suppliers because they're key players in any SME's net zero journey. Think of it like this: every pound an SME spends is a vote for the type of business world it wants to see. So, why not make that vote count?

Here's a practical approach for SMEs to embed sustainability criteria into procurement:

Create a shortlist of `Net Zero Heroes': These suppliers have demonstrated clear, credible sustainability commitments. By highlighting these businesses, SMEs make sustainable spending decisions straightforward and intuitive for the entire team.

Regularly engage with current suppliers: Encourage regular conversations about suppliers' net zero plans. Consistently asking this question can prompt suppliers to act sooner rather than later.

Prioritise suppliers with clear plans: Making sustainability an integral part of decision-making sends a strong message to the market: sustainability is a priority. This proactive stance also helps SMEs prepare for inevitable future requirements from larger clients.

Embedding sustainability into procurement aligns the team with broader net zero goals and makes it clear to suppliers that ignoring sustainability isn't an option. Small nudges today can lead to significant changes tomorrow. As accountants, the role here is clear: guiding SMEs to see procurement spending as an opportunity to influence positive change.

Empowering the Team—Ownership Beats Oversight Every Time

Having a plan is one thing, but executing it effectively is another. The key lies in empowering team members with clear responsibilities and ownership of specific net zero actions. Accountants advising SMEs don't have to take on every responsibility themselves. Nor should they default to the hard-pressed business owner or MD. Instead, they can help SMEs assign ownership to those best placed operationally to make progress.

The operations lead is well-placed to lead on many of these initiatives and report on progress. Similarly, if someone in an admin role is detail-oriented, assigning them supplier sustainability evaluations can bring quicker results. It's all about empowering team members to take ownership.

Here's how SMEs can approach it:

Encourage clear delegation: Delegating tasks based on interest and proximity to the action ensures practical ownership. It transforms abstract plans into concrete achievements.

Rotate responsibilities: Periodic rotation keeps initiatives fresh, prevents fatigue, and builds broader awareness and skills in sustainability across the entire team.

Celebrate achievements: Acknowledging successful ownership motivates continued engagement. Regular recognition reinforces the importance of sustainability efforts, building team confidence and momentum.

By promoting clear accountability through team ownership, accountants help SMEs turn their net zero plans from intentions into real, impactful results. And that's what it's all about, making sustainability a collective, achievable mission rather than just another task on the to-do list.

The 90-Day Review Cycle: Staying Agile and On-Track

Have you ever noticed how quickly well-intended plans can get sidelined? We've all been there. That's why the magic of accountability really happens in the consistent check-ins. Think of your net zero plan like any other key business goal; quarterly reviews keep the momentum alive.

Every 90 days, bring your team together for a straightforward, honest progress chat. Ask these three simple questions:

- **What's worked?** Celebrate any wins, no matter how small. It keeps the energy positive.
- **What's not working?** Be open. Identify roadblocks or where you might be off track.
- **What needs tweaking?** Make immediate, realistic adjustments based on your findings.

Why 90 days? It's short enough to keep actions front-of-mind and stop procrastination creeping in, yet long enough to see meaningful progress or adapt if circumstances change.

Crucially, these sessions aren't about blaming or shaming, but about openness, learning, and practical next steps. Make this part of your regular meeting rhythm, just like reviewing financials. The 'holding-to-account concept' is both skewed and unhelpful.

We're only really accountable to ourselves. Let's be honest, we have complete freedom to choose whether to do something. What we **can** do with our teams is mutually agree on what to prioritise, while still maintaining momentum towards achieving our targets.

And here's the beauty of it: by making the net zero review a regular event, it quickly becomes a habit rather than a chore. It's just part of what you do. Each review gives you a chance to:

- Celebrate what's working (positive feedback is fuel for engagement)
- Adjust the course without stress if things aren't going as planned
- Keep the conversation about sustainability fresh and relevant internally

Regular, easy-going reviews like this are your best tool to ensure your SME's net zero ambitions stay on track and become a reality, not just good intentions on paper.

Summary

So, you've set your ambition, figured out your actions, and laid out accountability, but execution is where the rubber truly hits the road. Plans are great, but they only make a difference when they're consistently put into action. For SMEs, execution is about embedding net zero seamlessly into daily business activities, leveraging their influence wisely through procurement, and empowering team members by giving them ownership of specific initiatives.

Our role as accountants, whether internal or external advisors, isn't just to measure progress; it's to champion a mindset where net zero becomes part of the everyday business routine. The practical magic happens when simple, regular habits align with clear accountability, keeping net zero on the agenda week after week, month after month, year after year.

Remember, flexibility is essential. Regular 90-day reviews paired with annual published updates ensure the plan remains relevant, actionable, and realistic. Don't chase perfection; embrace progress, celebrate small wins, and openly acknowledge any setbacks. This transparency builds trust and credibility with stakeholders, demonstrating genuine commitment rather than merely ticking boxes.

And now, with a practical execution approach firmly in place, you're ideally positioned to turn your experience into valuable advisory conversations with SME clients. That's precisely where we're heading next in Chapter 9. How to transform everything you've learned into an impactful advisory offering that adds value.

CHAPTER 9

NET ZERO AS A SERVICE

By now, we've established that accountants have a unique vantage point when guiding SMEs on their net zero journeys. You've seen how your existing skills, like analysing data, forecasting outcomes, and advising on strategic decisions, already align perfectly with the sustainability challenge.

So, what's next? Well, we're taking all that groundwork and turning it into a practical service offering, Net Zero as a Service, or NZaaS. Think of this as a natural extension of what you already do, tailored specifically for SMEs who, unlike big corporations, don't have dedicated sustainability teams or budgets to bring in specialist consultants.

This isn't just another advisory service; it's an opportunity to genuinely help SMEs navigate an increasingly crucial area affecting their bottom line and their future viability. With net zero becoming a non-negotiable requirement, especially within supply chains, SMEs already face pressure from clients and regulators to show real progress. Who better to step up and support them than you, the accountant, who already knows their business inside out?

This chapter isn't simply an invitation to consider enhancing your service offering; it's a call to action. It lies at the heart of this book's title:

`Catalyst: How Accountants Can Be the Agents of Change in the Net Zero Transition'

We'll build on everything we've covered so far and explore exactly how you can structure, market, and deliver NZaaS effectively. We'll get practical, providing you with the tools, insights, and confidence to make this a seamless part of your advisory toolkit.

Structuring Your NZaaS Offering

Delivering **Net Zero as a Service (NZaaS)** is all about structure, but it doesn't have to be rigid. Think of it like any strategic planning session, but with a clear focus on helping your client navigate their unique net zero journey. Each step you take builds on the one before it, guiding the process to make it smooth, educational, and highly productive. The beauty of this approach is in its simplicity and clarity.

But let's not forget that the process needs to be flexible to meet the client where they are. That's why it's important to have different service tiers that cater to clients at varying stages of their net zero journey. We can keep it straightforward and, most importantly, relevant.

Step 1: Prework and Initial Carbon Assessment

Before you sit down with your client, getting a clear snapshot of where they stand is essential. This is where the power of a high-level, spend-based emissions assessment comes in. Using a carbon accounting tool, you quickly identify key sources of emissions within the business. Think of it as a health check, not just for the business, but for their sustainability journey.

Now, this initial assessment does more than just provide a number. It sets the stage for the client's engagement by educating them on their current emissions and pointing out the low-hanging fruit for improvement. You're not only setting expectations but also positioning yourself as the guide through this process.

Client Benefit: When you sit down for your first honest discussion, your client is informed. They understand why net zero planning is crucial and are ready to dig in.

Accountant Benefit: You enter the next phase with a prepared client, which means you can jump straight into meaningful planning. The groundwork is laid, making your job smoother and faster.

Step 2: Client Insight Session

This session is where the magic happens. With the initial data, you sit down for a collaborative session with your client. You'll review the findings, validate the results, and address any surprises. The idea here is to have an open conversation that isn't just about reviewing numbers; it's about building trust, getting their buy-in, and understanding their unique business challenges.

By the end of this session, you want your client to feel heard, understood, and confident in the next steps. The insight you gather will form the foundation for realistic priorities and actionable targets.

Client Benefit: The client feels like this process is *theirs*. They aren't being handed a one-size-fits-all plan. They're co-authoring their strategy.

Accountant Benefit: You now have a clearer understanding of their current situation. The session gives you valuable insight into what's working, what needs more focus, and where potential roadblocks might be.

Step 3: Strategic Planning Workshop

At this point, you're facilitating a workshop to create a practical, realistic 12-month action plan. Here, you'll help your client identify clear actions, assign responsibilities, and most importantly, agree on measurable KPIs. This step is crucial because it gives the client something tangible to work with, a roadmap that outlines what they need to do and when.

You're making the whole concept of net zero manageable. What seemed overwhelming before is now broken down into bite-sized actions. By the end of the workshop, your client has a clear plan they can act on, and they know who is doing what.

Client Benefit: The client walks away with clarity, understanding the roles and responsibilities within their team, and a plan for making real progress.

Accountant Benefit: This is your sweet spot as an accountant. You're in your element, using your planning, budgeting, and forecasting skills to shape an actionable strategy aligned with their business goals.

Step 4: Implementation Support and 90-Day Check-Ins

Planning is fantastic, but execution is where the rubber meets the road. Regular 90-day check-ins become invaluable. You'll track progress, celebrate wins, address challenges, and adjust the plan if needed. These check-ins aren't just about holding the client accountable; they provide ongoing support, encouragement, and guidance.

And, even better, every 90 days isn't just about reviewing numbers. It's about deepening the relationship with your client. You're not just their accountant, you're a partner in their sustainability journey. These regular touchpoints build trust, and you'll naturally find opportunities to provide more value.

Client Benefit: These check-ins keep the client motivated and reassured. They know their investment in sustainability is being actively managed and tracked.

Accountant Benefit: Regular check-ins allow you to stay closely connected, which opens up opportunities for further advisory services, whether that's refining strategies, offering new insights, or helping them adjust as their business evolves.

Step 5: Annual Review and Adjustment

At the end of the 12-month cycle, it's time for a big-picture review. You'll look back at what was achieved, discuss the lessons learned, and refine the strategy for the following year. This annual review ensures that the net zero plan remains aligned with the business's evolving priorities.

The annual review is where you truly demonstrate your value. You're not just checking a box; you're helping the business evolve its sustainability strategy to stay relevant and practical.

Client Benefit: Clients can see the impact of their efforts, making it easier to stay committed to continuous improvement. They understand what's working and where they need to refine their approach.

Accountant Benefit: You've demonstrated tangible value over the year, deepening your relationship and strengthening your position as a long-term strategic advisor.

Service Tiers for NZaaS Offering (Tailored for SMEs)

To make NZaaS work for your clients, offering different service tiers allows them to choose what's right for them. Most accountants will find the **Mid-Tier Package** the sweet spot, but offering a range of options helps you meet clients where they are in their net zero journey.

1. **Entry-Level Package:** This is for businesses just starting out. It's simple and straightforward, just the basics to get them started on their sustainability journey.

- **What's Included**: Prework and Initial Carbon Assessment, one Client Insight Session, basic action plan.
- **Client Benefit**: A clear starting point without overwhelming them. It's perfect for businesses that need to dip their toes into the world of net zero.

- **Accountant Benefit**: An easy package to sell to clients who need a low-touch, entry-level service.

2. **Mid-Tier Package:** This is where meaningful progress happens. This package goes deeper for businesses ready to take things up a notch, providing a 12-month plan and regular check-ins to track progress.

- **What's Included**: Everything in the Entry-Level Package, Full Strategic Planning Workshop, 12-month Net Zero Action Plan, Quarterly Check-ins, ongoing email support.
- **Client Benefit**: Clients get a comprehensive plan with measurable actions and ongoing support to stay on track.
- **Accountant Benefit**: This package aligns well with most accountants' core capabilities. It provides the structure for deeper engagement while keeping things manageable.

3. **Specialisation Opportunity: Sustainability Consultancy:** For accountants who want to take it a step further, sustainability consultancy is an option to explore. This tier is for those who want to fully integrate sustainability into their clients' operations, from finance to HR to procurement.

- **What's Included:** In-depth, bespoke services including advanced carbon reporting, full supply chain engagement, and tailored sustainability strategies.
- **Client Benefit**: A high-touch, fully integrated sustainability strategy that's unique to their business.

- **Accountant Benefit**: This is for accountants who want to specialise further in sustainability consultancy, opening up new revenue streams and solidifying their role as a strategic advisor.

Building Out a Specialism in Sustainability Consultancy

If you feel inspired, this service level can be a natural next step, but it's not for everyone. It requires deeper expertise and ongoing education, but it could be a great choice if you're passionate about sustainability and want to position yourself as a leader in this field. The world of sustainability is vast, and there's room for accountants to lead the way, but it's essential to acknowledge that it's a choice you can make based on your ambitions.

The 'Red Thread'—Making It Cohesive

What makes NZaaS truly powerful is its simplicity and the clarity you offer to your clients. The process doesn't need to be overwhelming; it's about clear communication, structured guidance, and ongoing engagement. Every step you take together reinforces their confidence, accountability, and ultimately their action. When it all comes together, your NZaaS offering isn't just a service; it's a strategic partnership, built on trust and a shared commitment to achieving meaningful, impactful change.

Marketing NZaaS Effectively

Marketing your new Net Zero as a Service (NZaaS) shouldn't feel like traditional marketing; it should be more like starting friendly, meaningful conversations. You're not pushing another product; you're inviting your clients into an exciting journey toward a brighter, more resilient future. This is your chance to help them get ahead of sustainability trends, stand out from competitors, and do something genuinely impactful without feeling overwhelmed.

Start where you already have trust: your existing relationships. These clients know you, trust your guidance, and they'll naturally listen when you suggest something new. Keep it relaxed. Ask casual questions like, 'Have you thought much about net zero? Are any customers or suppliers bringing it up? Want a quick snapshot of where you're at?' It's just a conversation starter, no hard sell.

Remember, businesses don't always embrace change because they want to; sometimes, they have to. Maybe they're feeling pressure from customers, regulators, or their supply chain, or perhaps they spot opportunities, like cutting costs, differentiating themselves in the market, or attracting environmentally conscious customers.

Clearly explain how your NZaaS offering simplifies managing these external pressures and turns sustainability into a genuine competitive advantage. Share relatable success stories, even if initially they're from outside your immediate client base. SMEs appreciate hearing how similar businesses achieved measurable benefits like cost savings or winning new contracts. Don't worry if you're starting without these stories; we'll soon discuss how you can quickly build your own compelling case studies.

When you talk about sustainability, avoid jargon. Keep it simple, clear, and reassuring. Let your clients know you'll guide them through every step, ensuring this doesn't become yet another thing on their already-full plates.

Easy, practical marketing actions can boost your visibility quickly. Informal webinars, bite-sized case studies, or quick tips shared on social media or email work wonders. And never underestimate personal referrals from happy clients; they're incredibly powerful.

For efficiency, do a quick, informal segmentation of your clients based on easily accessible clues. Consumer-facing businesses might be motivated by public image, while B2B firms might be pressured by their supply chains. Glancing at a client's website or LinkedIn can reveal much about their current sustainability stance.

After that quick check, clarify their needs with relaxed conversations. Ask them gently about their understanding of sustainability, external pressures, and internal goals like cost savings or branding improvements. Explore if they're ready to invest resources and see if they've made any sustainability moves. These friendly chats help position your NZaaS offer as the tailored support they need.

Now you're ready to frame conversations effectively. Acknowledge their specific circumstances, like supply chain pressure or brand opportunities, and introduce NZaaS as an easy, practical solution. Keep things reassuring and relatable, making it clear you'll be their partner every step of the way, turning curiosity into action.

Selling NZaaS Confidently

Moving from friendly conversations to actual commitment doesn't have to feel awkward. You're not selling, you're guiding clients toward something genuinely valuable. The trick to confidently selling NZaaS is simply making clear connections between the service and the benefits your clients care about most.

When clients raise concerns about time, resources, or complexity, see these as chances to reassure. Emphasise how your structured, straightforward approach simplifies the journey toward net zero, breaking everything down into clear steps and achievable milestones.

Talk confidently and enthusiastically about tangible benefits they'll quickly see, like cost savings, enhanced brand reputation, and better supplier relationships. Highlight easy first steps and quick wins, keeping the energy positive and reassuring them that NZaaS is manageable and rewarding.

The real secret to confident selling is authenticity. You're offering something constructive that aligns with your clients' needs. By being clear, honest, and approachable, your clients will naturally want to move forward.

Pricing Your NzaaS

Pricing doesn't have to be tricky, complicated, or uncomfortable. It simply needs to be clear, fair, and aligned with the value you offer. Your goal is to set prices that reflect the tangible benefits your clients will experience, feel accessible to SMEs, and ensure your service stays profitable.

Be upfront and transparent about what's included. You've got clearly defined service tiers, use these as your anchor. Clients appreciate simplicity and clarity. Keep the pricing structure straightforward so it's easy to understand what they're getting and why it's valuable.

Instead of charging purely by time, consider a value-based approach. Tie your price directly to clear, relatable outcomes like saving money, winning new customers, or easing compliance pressures. For example, you might say, `With our mid-tier package, you'll get a clear emissions baseline, practical action plans, quarterly progress checks, and ongoing support, giving you measurable business advantages from day one.'

The best pricing conversations happen when clients see the link between cost and value. Be confidently transparent, anchor your prices in real-world outcomes, and reassure your clients they're making a smart, strategic investment. This open, informal, and clear approach reinforces trust, positioning you as their go-to advisor on sustainability.

Building Strategic Partnerships

You don't have to do it all alone. Building strategic partnerships is one of the smartest moves you can make when growing your NZaaS offering. Partnerships not only amplify your impact but also enhance your credibility and reach. Think of them as extensions of your team, experts in areas complementary to your strengths.

Start by looking at professionals or businesses whose skills naturally complement yours, such as environmental consultants, sustainability software providers, or even renewable energy specialists. These partners bring additional depth to your service without you needing to become an expert in every aspect.

When approaching potential partners, keep conversations straightforward and mutual. Highlight how working together brings clear, shared benefits, more business opportunities, stronger client offerings, and broader networks. Informal chats or joint webinars can be an easy way to test compatibility and build trust.

Effective partnerships are built on clarity and mutual respect. Be upfront about expectations, roles, and how you'll manage client interactions. The right partnerships broaden your service and deepen the value your clients experience, helping you become their trusted advisor across a broader range of sustainability solutions.

Continuous Professional Development (CPD)

Sustainability evolves rapidly, but staying informed doesn't need to be overwhelming. Keeping your knowledge fresh can be straightforward, enjoyable, and empowering, ensuring you stay ahead confidently.

Focus on quality rather than quantity in your education. Subscribe to trusted industry newsletters, podcasts, or webinars that deliver insights enjoyably. Networking with peers and partners can provide valuable perspectives through casual conversations.

Attend workshops or seminars selectively, choosing topics directly relevant to your clients or personal interests. This targeted approach keeps expertise sharp without overload.

Continuous learning isn't just about keeping up; it's about staying inspired. Approach it as a chance to enhance your advisory skills, reinforce your credibility, and maintain the value and relevance of your NZaaS offering.

Summary

In this chapter, we've explored practical ways to structure, market, sell, and price your NZaaS offering effectively, leveraging strategic partnerships and maintaining your professional edge. You've seen how straightforward conversations, authentic selling, clear pricing, and targeted education can make your NZaaS offering valuable and appealing.

But what if you're wondering how to create those initial, compelling success stories that resonate with potential clients? That's where we're headed next. In Chapter 10, we'll explore how you can become your own first NZaaS client, gathering authentic experiences and powerful stories to demonstrate credibility and inspire your clients.

CHAPTER 10

YOUR FIRST CLIENT IS YOU!

Be your own test case.

At this final stage of the book, I'm hoping you've started to see yourself not just as an accountant but as a **catalyst**. If you look at the position of accountants in the global economy, we have a remarkable vantage point. We're uniquely positioned to influence and accelerate meaningful change across a vast swathe of global business emissions, namely, amongst SMEs. Individually, each small business might feel their contribution is minor, yet collectively, SMEs represent a significant portion of the world's emissions. They're influential, too. Employees in SMEs have a much clearer view of what the business is doing, and they're more likely to be directly involved in net zero initiatives. So, perhaps inspired to make lifestyle changes that align and seem part of something bigger.

Amongst the general population, relatively few of us have the potential to create meaningful, wide-ranging impact across entire sectors and supply chains. We accountants do. We hold trusted relationships with countless SMEs, and through those connections, we can multiply positive action far beyond the scope of our businesses.

So, that leaves us with a big responsibility and an opportunity. If we don't step up and help SMEs transition to net zero, who else realistically will?

But before we can credibly guide others, we must experience the journey ourselves. That's what this chapter is about: becoming your own first NZaaS client. It's about putting everything we've discussed into practice, within your own business first. Trust me, once you start this journey yourself, you won't just feel inspired, you'll feel empowered. You'll move from thinking about net zero as a daunting external requirement to feeling it's achievable, rewarding, and deeply aligned with your values as an accountant.

So, let's take this final step together. I'll share my personal journey and the real-life insights I gained, revisiting the genuine surprises that challenged some of my early assumptions. I'll also share what it was like taking my first pilot clients through the process and how experiencing it firsthand has helped me better understand the unique role we accountants have as the catalyst that SMEs genuinely need.

Reality Check: Moving from Control to Influence

When I initially started thinking seriously about our business's carbon footprint, I assumed we had everything under control. After all, accountants are used to clarity, control, and measurable outcomes. But net zero quickly challenged my assumptions in a big way.

It didn't take long to realise that our emissions weren't just down to us. I was suddenly dependent on our suppliers' actions, or lack thereof, in decarbonising their own operations. Even closer to home, our hybrid-working employees introduced unexpected complexity. Their commuting choices and home-office setups affected our carbon footprint in ways we hadn't fully appreciated initially.

The biggest reality check was recognising that business growth directly opposed absolute emissions reductions. As we grew, our emissions naturally increased, despite our best efforts. It wasn't something I'd considered, and it quickly became clear that absolute emissions targets alone weren't realistic for growing businesses. Now, let's be clear: the overarching requirement of net zero is ultimately about absolute emissions reduction, and understandably, some might find it controversial to shift focus away from absolute figures. I've agonised over this dilemma of what is required of us all to combat climate change versus targeting much smaller impacts we can make, hoping to catalyse that change. Pragmatically speaking, as accountants advising SMEs, our job is to work effectively within the reality we face today, using the tools and metrics that make meaningful progress achievable.

This realisation led me to rethink the way we measure progress. Instead of absolute figures, intensity metrics like emissions per employee or per unit of revenue became incredibly valuable. These metrics weren't just more realistic; they were ethically sound. They allowed us to communicate our progress honestly without stalling growth or sacrificing our values.

Net zero taught me much about letting go of strict control and embracing influence instead. It showed me how crucial collaboration with employees, suppliers, and peers is and made clear just how much accountants like us can shape the broader conversation around sustainability. And that's what makes our role so important, and exciting.

Piloting NZaaS: Bringing Theory to Life

When piloting NZaaS, my first step was to test the approach within my own business. Doing so immediately highlighted practical challenges and nuances that theory alone couldn't capture. From choosing carbon accounting tools to interpreting complex emissions data, every step offered tangible insights and reinforced the value of hands-on experience.

With our pilot complete, I confidently took the NZaaS approach to my first external pilot clients, two agency-style SMEs, one a certified B Corp and the other B Corp-curious. Both businesses were similar to my own, with a hybrid workplace approach and business-to-business (B2B) service-focused operations.

Because I'd already navigated many of the initial hurdles internally, the pilot clients experienced a smoother transition. However, engaging with them reinforced how critical clarity and simplicity were in every communication. What had become second nature to me, like the necessity of intensity metrics or realistic emissions targets, required careful explanation and reassurance.

Piloting NZaaS with these real-world clients validated much of my earlier thinking. It underscored the necessity of translating complex sustainability concepts into clear, actionable steps. Above all, these pilot experiences affirmed that our role isn't merely about providing solutions but guiding clients through uncertainty with empathy, practicality, and genuine understanding.

Supply Chain Engagement: Navigating Real-World Challenges

When it came time to engage our supply chain, I wasn't entirely sure what responses I'd get, but honestly, nothing came as a huge surprise. Despite our close working relationships, our smaller suppliers often didn't reply at all, probably uncertain about how to start their sustainability conversations. Conversely, larger suppliers usually provided vague, high-level statements about their commitment to sustainability without concrete actions to back them up, though publicly listed companies like Xero and Sage were notable exceptions, having clear and detailed sustainability information readily available.

These experiences taught me an important lesson: supply chain engagement isn't about making considerable demands or expecting immediate transformations. Instead, it's about starting meaningful conversations, building trust, and providing gentle, ongoing encouragement. Our role as accountants is less about forcing rapid compliance and more about patiently nudging our suppliers towards greater transparency and action.

Approaching suppliers in this empathetic, collaborative manner led to more productive conversations. It reminded me that genuine, lasting change often begins quietly, with patient guidance rather than rigid demands. The great thing is that as more accountants have these conversations and consistently ask suppliers about their sustainability plans, momentum naturally builds. Imagine companies like Dext receiving multiple queries from key accounting partners. They'll soon understand that they need a better answer. Even bigger businesses can be nudged into meaningful change through the collective influence of SMEs.

CONCLUSION

Sir David Attenborough famously said of the climate crisis, `It is now a communications problem.' If you've reached this point, I hope you see that accountants, people just like you, are powerful and hugely influential communicators, too.

I've deliberately isolated net zero from the broader climate crisis throughout the book. Right at the beginning, I shared my certainty that the climate crisis is real, urgent, and driven by human activity. However, acknowledging the crisis is just the start; how we respond matters most. It's not enough to aim for net zero by 2050 and cross our fingers. Just like growing a business, how we get there matters every bit as much as reaching the final destination.

The financial world typically favours short-term thinking because of how we discount future events. A fossil fuel company's value might eventually collapse when demand falls away, but today's valuation methods downplay or ignore that risk because it seems so distant. As accountants, whether we work within SMEs or advise them externally, we're uniquely placed to confront these realities head-on, to have honest conversations, and to shift the focus toward longer-term, sustainable value.

We have to acknowledge that reaching net zero emissions means absolute reductions. Yet, practically, especially for SMEs, absolute cuts can feel overwhelming. The good news is, we don't need perfection. After all, it's called net zero, not absolute zero, for a reason. Accountants understand imperfection; we handle complexity every day. We can communicate that complexity clearly, turning daunting targets into realistic milestones that businesses can achieve step-by-step.

Why accountants, though? Think about it: SMEs represent 90% of global businesses, 60% of employment, and contribute around half of global GDP and emissions. Most net zero regulations don't directly apply to SMEs, so who else can they turn to for guidance they trust? Our role becomes critical. Whether you're embedded in the SME itself or, like us at Thrive, providing trusted external advice, you can help these businesses navigate the complexities of transitioning to net zero. We don't just crunch numbers; we translate numbers into meaningful action.

Of course, part of our role as communicators is helping SMEs avoid accusations of greenwashing. But that's easier than it might sound. Authenticity and transparency always win. Whether through formal IFRS sustainability disclosures, annual reports, or simple, straightforward storytelling, the message remains consistent: communicate where you are today, celebrate the progress you've made, and outline clearly the actions you intend to take next. Authenticity is persuasive, influential, and essential.

My invitation to you now is simple and practical: start today. Identify one explicit action you can take in your own business, or for the SMEs you advise, and then share it. Make your story relatable and inspiring. Every action you share can spark two more. Imagine creating a ripple effect, a climate-action Ponzi scheme of sorts, spreading rapidly through the countless SMEs around the globe.

You're welcome to follow my net zero journey on LinkedIn, where I regularly share the challenges, successes, and lessons we encounter at Thrive. I'd love to hear your stories, too. Visit our net-zero page at thrive.accountants for inspiration, and you'll find ideas for how your green credentials can authentically market your services.

Accountants like us have always supported growth, helping SMEs follow their instincts and dreams. Now, we have an even greater opportunity. Through clarity, empathy, and honest communication, we can help businesses thrive sustainably, not just in terms of profit but also in terms of their lasting impact on the planet.

Let's embrace our role as agents of change and step confidently forward, turning the daunting journey to net zero into something achievable, rewarding, and inspiring. Because accountants don't just report history; we can create it.

So let's go out there and show the world just how powerful accountants can truly be. Let's be catalysts, accelerating the green transition.

FURTHER INFORMATION/RESOURCES

These books offer valuable insights into achieving net zero emissions, the challenges and opportunities associated with addressing climate change, and the actions needed to create a sustainable future.

The Future We Choose: Surviving The Climate Crisis by Christiana Figueres and Tom Rivett-Carnac, Knopf (Penguin Random House, 2020).

Written by two architects of the Paris Agreement, this book outlines two possible scenarios for the future of our planet: one in which we fail to address the climate crisis adequately, and one in which we take action to limit global warming to 1.5 degrees Celsius.

Drawdown: The Most Comprehensive Plan Ever Proposed To Reverse Global Warming, edited by Paul Hawken, (Penguin Books, 2017).

This book comprehensively analyses the most effective solutions to combat climate change, ranked by their potential to reduce greenhouse gas emissions and reverse global warming.

The Green New Deal: Why the Fossil Fuel Civilization will collapse by 2028 and the Bold Economic Plan to Save Life on Earth, by Jeremy Rifkin (St. Martin's Press, 2019).

In this book, Jeremy Rifkin argues for a global Green New Deal as a transformative economic and environmental strategy to address climate change and transition to a sustainable future.

Net Zero: How We Stop Causing Climate Change, by Dieter Helm (Harper Collins, 2020).

Dieter Helm explores the concept of net zero and outlines practical strategies for achieving it, including technological innovations, policy reforms, and changes in individual behaviour.

How to Avoid a Climate Disaster: The Solutions We Have and the Breakthrough We Need, Bill Gates (Alfred A. Knop, imprint of Penguin Random House, 2021).

Bill Gates provides a comprehensive overview of the challenges posed by climate change and outlines practical solutions for achieving net zero emissions, drawing on insights from science, technology, economics, and policy.

Climate Capitalism: Capitalism in the Age of Climate Change, by L. Hunter Lovins and Boyd Cohen (Hill & Wang, 2011)

This book explores how businesses can thrive in a world increasingly impacted by climate change. It discusses innovative strategies for sustainable business practices, green technologies, and leveraging market forces to address environmental challenges.

The Sustainability Edge: How to Drive Top-Line Growth with Triple-Bottom-Line Thinking, by Suhas Apte and Jagdish N. Sheth (Wharton Digital Press, 2014).

This book focuses on the business case for sustainability and outlines strategies for integrating environmental and social considerations into business practices to drive innovation, reduce costs, and enhance brand reputation.

Websites:

The following resources offer valuable insights, tools, and guidance for accountants seeking to understand and address the accounting implications of net zero initiatives, climate-related risks, and sustainability reporting requirements.

The Carbon Trust (carbontrust.com)

It offers a range of resources, guides, and tools to help businesses understand their carbon footprint, set emissions reduction targets, and implement strategies to achieve net zero. It provides carbon footprint calculators, energy efficiency advice, and information on renewable energy options.

Sustainable Small Business (sustainablesmallbusiness.com)

Provides practical guidance and resources for SMEs looking to adopt sustainable practices and reduce their environmental impact. They offer tips on energy efficiency, waste reduction, green procurement, and sustainable business operations.

Green Business Network (greenbusinessntework.org)

Resources, workshops, and networking opportunities for small businesses interested in sustainability and environmental responsibility. They offer guidance on green certification, eco-friendly practices, and sustainable business models.

Sustainable Business Toolkit (sustainableusinesstoolkit.com)

Articles, case studies, and tools to help SMEs integrate sustainability into their business strategies. Topics covered include carbon management, sustainable supply chain management, and corporate social responsibility.

The SME Climate Hub (smeclimatehub.org)

An initiative that provides guidance, tools, and support for SMEs to take climate action and commit to net zero emissions. They offer a Net Zero Pledge and resources to help SMEs measure, reduce, and offset their carbon footprint.

B Lab (bcorporation.net)

Resources for businesses interested in becoming Certified B Corporations, which meet rigorous standards of social and environmental performance, transparency, and accountability. They provide guidance on sustainability reporting, impact assessment, and best practices for responsible business.

Carbon Disclosure Project (cwp.net)

Provides tools and resources for companies and investors to measure, disclose, and manage environmental impacts, including carbon emissions. Accountants can access CDP's reports, guidance documents, and case studies on climate-related disclosure.

The Task Force on Climate-related Financial Disclosures (fsb-tcfd.org)

guidance for companies on disclosing climate-related financial risks and opportunities in their financial filings. Accountants can access TCFD's recommendations, implementation guides, and resources for integrating climate-related disclosures into financial reporting.

ACKNOWLEDGEMENTS

I'd like to thank the team at Sage for their invaluable support throughout this project. They not only provided technical guidance on key concepts but also acted as a sounding board as I developed my thinking. Their brilliantly supportive approach helped me clarify important ideas and stay aligned with broader market developments.

I am especially grateful for the opportunity to access their climate scientists, whose expertise added real depth to the book. A particular thanks goes to Richard Fitzherbert for his detailed beta-read feedback. His generosity with time and insight went above and beyond, and made a significant difference to the quality of the book.

Beta Readers

My thanks also go to the following beta readers, who gave their time and perspectives to strengthen the book:

Richard Fitzherbert, Sage
Mathias Karady, Sage
Adam Bastock, Small 99
Karen Reyburn, WeArePF

Marianne Dadd, MD Accountancy
Monika Kamycka, Oppic
Stephen Gibbens, Accountech Solutions

And finally, to the burgeoning community of sustainability-minded accountants and bookkeepers who keep me grounded, motivated, inspired, hopeful, and (Kathyrn, Scott, Penny) laughing.

THE AUTHOR

James Lizars is the founder of Thrive, a finance and accounting business dedicated to helping innovative companies grow with clarity, confidence, and purpose. A Chartered Certified Accountant, James has spent over three decades working with small and medium-sized enterprises, combining deep technical expertise with a passion for people and the planet.

At Thrive, James leads a team of committed finance professionals who go beyond the numbers. Their work not only delivers robust accounting and finance operations, but also helps clients navigate complex challenges such as scaling internationally, accessing investment, and embedding sustainability into strategy.

James is a council member of ACCA (the Association of Chartered Certified Accountants), where he champions the role of accountants as advisors and change-makers. He believes accountants are uniquely placed to influence how small businesses approach net zero, and he advocates for the profession to embrace this responsibility with confidence and creativity.

Through his writing, speaking, and advisory work, James promotes the B Corp philosophy demonstrating that businesses can achieve commercial success while driving positive impact for stakeholders and society.

When he's not immersed in growing Thrive as a better business-case study, James enjoys family life, mountain biking, and the occasional adventure that takes him outside his comfort zone. His mission remains clear: to inspire and equip accountants to play a central role in building a fairer, more sustainable future.

https://www.linkedin.com/in/jameslizars/

https://jameslizars.com/

Printed in Dunstable, United Kingdom

80007913R00087